# Catalyst

## Accelerating Perl Web Application Development

Design, develop, test and deploy applications with the open-source Catalyst MVC framework

**Jonathan Rockway**

[PACKT] PUBLISHING

BIRMINGHAM - MUMBAI

# Catalyst

## Accelerating Perl Web Application Development



First published: December 2007

Production Reference: 1031207

Published by Packt Publishing Ltd.
32 Lincoln Road
Olton
Birmingham, B27 6PA, UK.

ISBN 978-1-847190-95-6

www.packtpub.com

Cover Image by Raghuram Ashok (raghuram@iiitb.ac.in)

# Credits

**Author**
Jonathan Rockway

**Reviewers**
K. Jamie Cheetham
Joshua A. McAdams

**Senior Acquisition Editor**
Douglas Paterson

**Development Editor**
Nikhil Bangera

**Technical Editor**
Swapna V. Verlekar
Usha Iyer

**Editorial Team Leader**
Mithil Kulkarni

**Project Manager**
Abhijeet Deobhakta

**Indexer**
Hemangini Bari

**Proofreader**
Harminder Singh

**Production Coordinator**
Shantanu Zagade

**Cover Designer**
Shantanu Zagade

# About the Author

**Jonathan Rockway**, a member of the Catalyst Core Team, has been programming Perl since his middle school years. He became professionally involved with Perl when we was a desktop support minion at the University of Chicago and inherited a mod_perl application. He now works as a software developer at Infinity Interactive. In his spare time, he maintains a collection of modules on the CPAN and tries to speak at as many Perl conferences as possible.

# About the Reviewers

**Kieran Jamie Cheetham** is currently residing in the UK and graduated university with a first class masters degree in Physics, Astrophysics and Cosmology.

After spending a number of years working on small HTML/CSS projects, he started working for an open source software company in northwest England. Initially focusing on refactoring PHP web-based administration interfaces and dealing with domain name management he moved on to MVC systems in Perl—and in particular Catalyst.

When not working Kieran enjoys exploring the countryside, pointing his telescopes to the night sky, reading science fiction and tinkering with machines.

I would like to thank Matt for helping open my eyes to some of the "wonders" of Perl, American clients keeping me company when hacking all through the night, L and B for helping to keep me sane, and all of the various people on IRC who were willing to answer my inane questions and help test and document some of my work.

**Joshua McAdams** is a programmer who loves hacking Perl as well as talking about programming on Perlcast, the Perl podcast. He is a CPAN contributor, a two-time YAPC host, and a winner of the Perl Foundation's White Camel Award. For a day-job, he works at Performics, a division of DoubleClick, where he serves as Engineering Manager for the Data Warehousing team.

I'd like to thank the Perl community for their continuing creation and innovation. This is a great community to be a part of. Though I've been coding for many years, I've became a much better programmer in these last few years that I've been an active member of the Perl world. I would encourage everyone who works in Perl to be a part of the community by attending a PM meeting, visiting a weekend workshop or YAPC, or just hanging out on `irc.perl.org`, `perlmonks.org`, `use.perl.org`, or any of the many other Perl haunts.

# Table of Contents

**Preface** 1

**Chapter 1: Introduction to Catalyst** 5

**Catalyst Application Architecture** 6

Extensibility 7

Reusability 8

Flexibility 8

Reliability 8

**Installing Catalyst** 9

CPAN 9

**Where to go for Help?** 10

**Summary** 11

**Chapter 2: Creating a Catalyst Application** 13

**Creating the Application Skeleton** 13

**MyApp Directory Structure** 17

Files in the MyApp Directory 18

Files in the lib Directory 18

Files in the root Directory 19

Files in the script Directory 19

Files in the t Directory 20

**Adding a View** 20

Using a Template To Render the Page 25

Some Technical Details 26

**Adding a Database** 27

Installing SQLite 27

Creating a Database Schema 28

Creating a Database Model for Catalyst 28

Using the Model 29

**Summary** 30

**Chapter 3: Building a Real Application** 31
**Environment Setup** 32
**Database Design** 32
**Understanding the Interface to the Database** 34
**TTSite** 37
Creating the Index Page 38
Creating a "Not Found" Page 38
**Viewing People** 40
**Basic CRUD** 43
**Forms** 43
**Finishing Up** 47
**Summary** 51
**Chapter 4: Expanding the Application** 53
**Configuration Files** 53
Configuring the Address Book 55
**Sessions** 56
Adding Sessions to the Address Book 57
Sessions in the Database 59
**Using Components from Outside Catalyst** 60
**Searching and Paging** 64
**Authentication and Authorization** 72
Authentication 72
Authorization 73
Adding Authentication and Authorization to the Address Book 75
**Summary** 82
**Chapter 5: Building a More Advanced Application** 83
**The Application** 83
Background 83
**Creating the Database** 84
Populating the Database 88
**Extracting the Data** 92
Chained ResultSets 95
Custom ResultSets 97
**Putting the Data on the Web** 99
**Summary** 117
**Chapter 6: Building Your Own Model** 119
**Extending a DBIx::Class Model** 119
Custom Methods Without Raw SQL 121
Calling Database Functions 121
**Creating a Database Model from Scratch** 122
**Implementing a Filesystem Model** 124

Tweaking the Model 128
Request Context Inside the Model 129
Maintainable Models 130
Other Components 132
**Summary** **132**
**Chapter 7: Hot Web Topics** **133**
**REST** **133**
Getting some REST 134
REST Controller 135
REST Authentication 135
Adding an Entity 136
REST Easy 143
**AJAX** **144**
Getting Started 144
Jemplate 144
Implementing AJAX 146
**RSS** **151**
**Summary** **153**
**Chapter 8: Testing** **155**
**Mechanics** **156**
**Testing ChatStat** **158**
Testing a Database 159
Testing the Web Interface 161
**Testing the Address Book** **165**
Logging In 165
Testing Forms 167
Testing JavaScript 169
**Summary** **173**
**Chapter 9: Deployment** **175**
**Basics** **175**
PAR Deployment 177
Configuration Management 178
**Configuring a Web Server** **178**
Apache 179
FastCGI 179
Static Content 180
mod_perl 180
Performance Considerations 181
Development Server and perlbal 182
**Summary** **183**
**Index** **185**

# Preface

Many web applications are implemented in a way that makes developing them painful and repetitive. Catalyst is an open-source Perl-based Model-View-Controller framework that aims to solve this problem by reorganizing your web application to design and implement it in a natural, maintainable and testable manner, making web development fun, fast and rewarding.

Everything that your web application needs to do is only written once; you connect to the database in one place, have configuration in one place, etc. Then, you just write actions for each URL that your application needs, without worrying about the database connections or HTML to produce. Catalyst will handle the details so you can worry about writing your application. Catalyst is designed to be reliable. There are hundreds of production applications and thousands of users. The code is well-tested, and new releases almost always maintain compatibility with applications written for older versions. You don't have to worry about Catalyst breaking your application and slowing down your development. It just works. Most importantly, Catalyst has a thriving community. You can ask a question on the IRC channel and get a response at almost any time of the day.

This book helps you understand the Catalyst framework, its MVC architecture and also provides detailed walkthroughs to create your web applications. Using this book you can build, test and deploy a site with Catalyst and also learn how to extend Catalyst through plug-ins.

## What This Book Covers

*Chapter 1* serves as an introduction to Catalyst and its features. You will also learn how to install and get it up and running.

In *Chapter 2*, we will create a Catalyst application skeleton, step through the different files in its directories, and learn how to generate HTML output and connect a SQLite database to Catalyst.

In *Chapter 3* we build our first real application - the address book. We learn to design and understand the "CRUD" interface to the database of our site and write some Catalyst actions.

In *Chapter 4*, we add common features to our address book application. We learn how to add sessions to our application programmed search logic and identify users and use their identity to control access to the application. Later, we explore authentication and authorization by implementing page-level and record-level access control.

We build a new application called ChatStat in *Chapter 5*. Here we explore the features of DBIC for easy handling of data and use Catalyst to get the data from DBIC onto the web.

In *Chapter 6* we look at the different ways to access the data model. We learn to write a database model and create a filesystem model from scratch, which is integrated with the Catalyst application.

In *Chapter 7*, we will develop a REST API to give the user easy access to our application's data. We also learn to add AJAX interactivity and incorporate RSS feeds in our application.

*Chapter 8* covers an important part of any project, i.e., testing. We learn to write programs to test our Catalyst application automatically. We see how to test the individual non-Catalyst components, and then the components inside Catalyst.

In *Chapter 9*, we learn to package our application and make it available as a PAR file, ready to run on a real web server.

# What You Need for This Book

Throughout this book, we will assume that you have the following packages installed and available:

- Perl version 5.8.1 or higher
- A working web server
- SQLite

# Conventions

In this book, you will find a number of styles of text that distinguish between different kinds of information. Here are some examples of these styles, and an explanation of their meaning.

There are three styles for code. Code words in text are shown as follows: "The best place for questions is the `#catalyst` IRC channel."

A block of code will be set as follows:

```
sub end : Private {
   my ($self, $c) = @_;
   $c->forward('View::TT');
}
```

Any command-line input and output is written as follows:

$ cpan -i DBD::SQLite DBIx::Class Catalyst::Model::DBIC::Schema

**New terms** and **important words** are introduced in a bold-type font. Words that you see on the screen, in menus or dialog boxes for example, appear in our text like this: "The MyApp directory structure shows the directories **lib**, **root**, **script**, and **t**."

> Important notes appear in a box like this.

> Tips and tricks appear like this.

## Reader Feedback

Feedback from our readers is always welcome. Let us know what you think about this book, what you liked or may have disliked. Reader feedback is important for us to develop titles that you really get the most out of.

To send us general feedback, simply drop an email to `feedback@packtpub.com`, making sure to mention the book title in the subject of your message.

If there is a book that you need and would like to see us publish, please send us a note in the **SUGGEST A TITLE** form on `www.packtpub.com` or email `suggest@packtpub.com`.

If there is a topic that you have expertise in and you are interested in either writing or contributing to a book, see our author guide on `www.packtpub.com/authors`.

# Customer Support

Now that you are the proud owner of a Packt book, we have a number of things to help you to get the most from your purchase.

## Downloading the Example Code for the Book

Visit `http://www.packtpub.com/files/code/0956_Code.zip`, and select this book from the list of titles to download any example code or extra resources for this book. The files available for download will then be displayed.

The downloadable files contain instructions on how to use them.

## Errata

Although we have taken every care to ensure the accuracy of our contents, mistakes do happen. If you find a mistake in one of our books—maybe a mistake in text or code—we would be grateful if you would report this to us. By doing this you can save other readers from frustration, and help to improve subsequent versions of this book. If you find any errata, report them by visiting `http://www.packtpub.com/support`, selecting your book, clicking on the **Submit Errata** link, and entering the details of your errata. Once your errata are verified, your submission will be accepted and the errata are added to the list of existing errata. The existing errata can be viewed by selecting your title from `http://www.packtpub.com/support`.

## Questions

You can contact us at `questions@packtpub.com` if you are having a problem with some aspect of the book, and we will do our best to address it.

# 1
# Introduction to Catalyst

Writing a web application is usually a repetitive process. For every page, you create a new script. This script performs essentially the same tasks as the other scripts in the application: connect to a database, get some input from the user, and produce a web page as the result. This style of application design results in a structure like this:

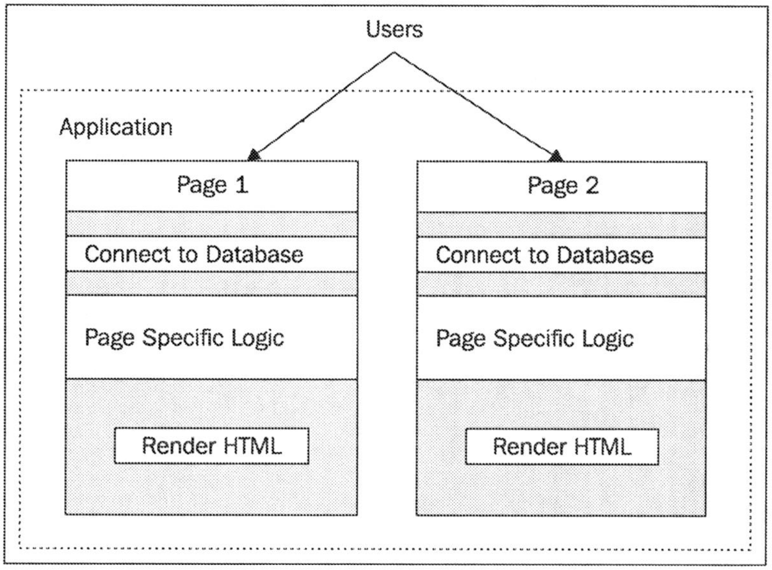


Building an application with this sort of design is certainly not a difficult process, but the constant repetition can be prone to error. If you decide to change your database, you will have to update the database connection string in each file. If you happen to forget one obscure file, you might not be aware until your users start sending you angry emails.

Of course, this problem is not limited to the database connection strings. As the diagram shows, repeated elements are everywhere. As each page generates its own HTML, a request from your web designer to update the layout of a page will involve having to dig through your Perl source code (potentially breaking database queries or other logic), just to change some HTML. In addition any time you make a change that affects your entire site or application, you'll have to make the change a number of times; once for each "page". Similarly, fixing one bug will entail copying the fix to every other place. This is inconvenient, a waste of time and just plain boring.

Catalyst is an open source Perl-based Model-View-Controller **framework** that aims to solve this problem by reorganizing your web application.

# Catalyst Application Architecture

Rather than making each location that a user may visit an individual file, we make each location an **action** inside a **Controller** class. Catalyst sits in front of each of these controllers, and when it receives a request, it dispatches the request to the proper action. When an action is called by the dispatcher, it's in a pre-configured environment—all configuration options have been read from a configuration file, all databases are connected, all parameters from the request have been parsed, etc. All your action has to do is implement the logic associated with the request; there is no setup that you have to manually perform.

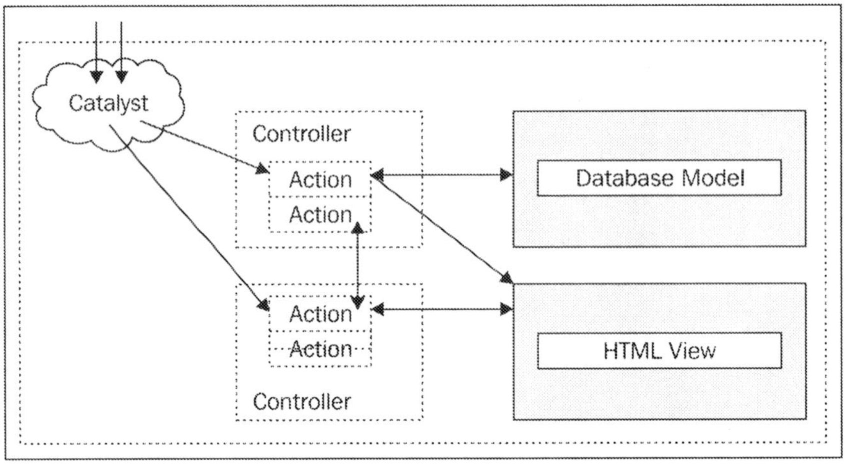


Although this dispatch mechanism is already an improvement over the traditional process, Catalyst doesn't stop here. Your actions can call on the help of **Models** and **Views**, as well.

A Model is a source of data. Most applications use a single relational database like MySQL or PostgreSQL as their Model, but Catalyst does not require that—you can use anything from files on disk, to an email server, or remote RSS feeds; and you can have as many Models as your application needs.

Each Model knows how to configure itself at startup (for example, connect to the database server), so you'll never have to worry about that. If you need to use a different database, you can change the connection information in one file, restart your application, and the change will take effect everywhere, automatically. The repetition that a traditional application would require is simply non-existent in Catalyst.

Lastly, a View is another component that your action may use. A View is a way to turn the raw data that your action generates into something more useful to your application's users. Typically, applications have a View that converts the data into an HTML page via a templating system, like the Template Toolkit, Mason, or ClearSilver.

Templating systems abstract your HTML or XML away from your Perl code, so the web designer can edit it without knowing anything about Perl or the underlying design of your application.

You don't have to completely understand what MVC is right now—we'll start learning the details in the next chapter. For now, think about all the code you've cut-n-pasted between files in your application and how Catalyst will eliminate that forever.

# Extensibility

MVC isn't all that Catalyst provides. At the time of writing, there were over 190 freely-available plugins that added new features to Catalyst. Existing plug-ins offer functionality such as configuration file parsers, specialized logging tools, email interfaces, caching, user authentication and authorization; cryptography, internationalization, and localization, browser detection and even virus scanning. Most of these plug-ins drop right into your application and instantly provide you with the advertised functionality. This saves you from having to reinvent the wheel for common (and uncommon!) tasks.

In addition to plug-ins, pre-made Models, Controllers, and Views (collectively called components) are also available. Since Catalyst is fully object-oriented, your application-specific components can simply "subclass" these off-the-shelf components and customize the functionality to whatever degree is necessary.

Finally, if there's no pre-built component available, there's the possibility that a generic Perl module from the CPAN (Comprehensive Perl Archive Network; `http://search.cpan.org/`) can help you—there are over 10,000 modules currently available!

# Reusability

Another advantage of Catalyst's MVC design is that the components need not be specific to one application. If you're developing a number of related applications, you can share components between them with minimal (or no) modification, since the components are just Perl objects that need not know anything specific about your application. (Of course, if you need a component that's specific to your application, that's no problem for Catalyst.)

# Flexibility

As Catalyst handles all the details of loading your components and handling requests, you aren't tied to any details of this process. This means that you can deploy your application with any web server (Apache and lighttpd are widely used) under whatever configuration best suits your environment. If you're using `mod_perl` with Apache 1.3, that's no problem for Catalyst. If you're using lighttpd as a proxy to several backend FastCGI servers, Catalyst will work great. Catalyst even comes with a built-in HTTP server, so you can develop applications without having to install and configure a web server.

With Catalyst, like Perl itself, *There Is More Than One Way To Do It*, and Catalyst will bend to fit your environment so you can use what you're already familiar with.

# Reliability

Finally, Catalyst is designed to be reliable. The run-time package comes with over 2600 unit tests that automatically check the reliability of Catalyst when you install it. In the unlikely event that there's something wrong with your Perl environment, Catalyst won't install until it's fixed. There's always the possibility of a bug in Catalyst, but nothing major has come up because the core developer team tries to keep Catalyst as small as possible. Everything that's non-essential is kept in plug-ins or in reusable base components. (We try to keep these stable too, of course.)

This reliability isn't just for the Catalyst developers though. When you create your application (or components within it), unit tests are automatically generated. These tests serve to make sure that your application is at least minimally functional. If you choose to, you can easily add your own automatic tests that can test every part of your application. Rather than manually going through your site when you make a major (or minor) change, you can have the computer double-check everything while you get a cup of coffee. Testing is examined in detail in Chapter 8.

# Installing Catalyst

Now that you're convinced that you want to try Catalyst, you just have to install it. Since Catalyst is Perl-based, you'll need to have a working version of Perl. Most Linux and BSD distributions come with a suitable Perl in the default install, as do many commercial Unix variants. (Mac OS X is no exception.) Microsoft Windows doesn't ship with Perl, but you can get a base Perl distribution for free from ActiveState, Strawberry Perl, or Cygwin. Regardless of your operating system, you'll need Perl version 5.8.1 or higher (5.8.8, the latest at the time of writing, is the version used in the book).

The easiest way to install Catalyst is via your operating system's package manager. This mostly applies to Linux and the BSDs and the syntax is specific to your distribution. On Debian-based versions of GNU/Linux, the command is:

```
$ apt-get install libcatalyst-perl
```

On FreeBSD or OpenBSD, you can build the Catalyst "port" by running the following commands as root:

```
$ cd /usr/ports/www/p5-Catalyst-Runtime
$ make install
```

If you're using ActiveState on Windows, ActiveState has a "PPM" package for Catalyst. You can find the PPM at `http://cpan.uwinnipeg.ca/dist/Catalyst-Runtime`.

Finally, be sure to check your operating system's manual for specific instructions on installing packages. The latest details are available from the Catalyst Installation guide at `http://search.cpan.org/perldoc?Catalyst::Manual::Installation`.

## CPAN

If your operating system doesn't provide pacakges, installing Catalyst directly from the CPAN is a simple process. Perl ships with a utility called `cpan` that handles the installation process for you. Simply run this from the command line:

```
$ cpan Catalyst::Runtime Catalyst::Devel
```

and Catalyst (and all of its dependencies) will be downloaded, integrity-checked and installed.

The disadvantage of this approach is that you'll need a C compiler `gcc`, `make`, and related development utilities. Most Linux distributions have these available, but they aren't a part of the default install. Mac OS X offers `gcc` and `make` as part of its "developer tools" package, which you'll need to install if you choose to use `cpan`.

The `cpan` script is, unfortunately, notorious for asking difficult questions the first time that you run it (in order to build a configuration suitable for your system). If you want to avoid these questions and just get Catalyst installed, try the `cat-install` script at `http://www.shadowcat.co.uk/static/cat-install`. You can download that file, run it with Perl, and Catalyst should be installed when it's finished running.

# Where to go for Help?

If `cpan` is just not working for you and you feel lost, the Catalyst community would love to help you out. The best place for questions is the `#catalyst` IRC channel on `irc.perl.org`. Users, developers, and other helpful people monitor this channel and are happy to answer Catalyst-related questions.

For longer questions, email is probably a better means of communication. Catalyst has an English-language users list that you can sign up for at: `http://lists.scsys.co.uk/cgi-bin/mailman/listinfo/catalyst`.

As Catalyst becomes more popular, new lists are being created for other languages. Catalyst-de was recently created for German-speaking users, and there's interest in creating a Japanese-language mailing list. Many readers of the English list speak other languages, so if you're having trouble with English, say so and someone can likely assist you in your native language.

Finally, the main project web site, `http://www.catalystframework.org/`, provides links to useful community tools including the Catalyst wiki, Planet Catalyst (a collection of Catalyst-related blog postings), and the Catalyst Advent Calendar (a mini-cookbook published each December).

As always, before posting to the mailing list or asking on IRC, do a quick Google search to see if you're experiencing a common problem.

# Summary

Many web applications are implemented in a way that makes developing them painful and repetitive. Catalyst, an MVC framework for Perl, lets you design and implement a web application in a natural, maintainable, and testable manner. Everything that your web application needs to do is only written once; you connect to the database in one place, have configuration in one place, etc. Then, you just write actions for each URL that your application needs, without worrying about the database connections or HTML to produce. Catalyst will handle the details so you can worry about writing your application. Thanks to Catalyst's plug-in system, it can do more than just dispatch requests—it can manage sessions and users for you, as well as handle many other common tasks. Catalyst is designed to be reliable. There are hundreds of production applications and thousands of users. The code is well-tested and new releases almost always maintain compatibility with applications written for older versions. You don't have to worry about Catalyst breaking your application and slowing down your development. It just works.

Most importantly, Catalyst (and Perl) has a thriving community. You can ask a question on the IRC channel and get a response at almost any time of the day. There are also resources on the web for learning more; blogs from developers and users, recipes on the advent calendar and a wealth of questions answered on the mailing list.

# 2
# Creating a Catalyst Application

Now that you've installed Catalyst, we are ready to create a simple application. In this chapter, we will be creating a basic application. We'll create the skeleton of the application and write some Catalyst actions. Then we'll learn how to use the Template Toolkit to generate HTML output and finally, connect a SQLite database to Catalyst with `DBIx::Class`.

## Creating the Application Skeleton

Catalyst comes with a script called `catalyst.pl` to make this task as simple as possible. `catalyst.pl` takes a single argument, the application's name, and creates an application of that name. The name can be any valid Perl module name, like `MyApp` or `MyCompany::HR::Timesheets`.

Let's get started by creating "`MyApp`", the example application for this chapter.

```
$ catalyst.pl MyApp
created "MyApp"
created "MyApp/"MyApp/script"
created "MyApp/lib"
created "MyApp/root"
created "MyApp/root/static"
created "MyApp/root/static/images"
created "MyApp/t"
created "MyApp/lib/MyApp"
created "MyApp/lib/MyApp/Model"
created "MyApp/lib/MyApp/View"
```

```
created "MyApp/lib/MyApp/Controller"
created "MyApp/myapp.yml"
created "MyApp/lib/MyApp.pm"
created "MyApp/lib/MyApp/Controller/Root.pm"
created "MyApp/README"
created "MyApp/Changes"
created "MyApp/t/01app.t"
created "MyApp/t/02pod.t"
created "MyApp/t/03podcoverage.t"
created "MyApp/root/static/images/catalyst_logo.png"
created "MyApp/root/static/images/btn_120x50_built.png"
created "MyApp/root/static/images/btn_120x50_built_shadow.png"
created "MyApp/root/static/images/btn_120x50_powered.png"
created "MyApp/root/static/images/btn_120x50_powered_shadow.png"
created "MyApp/root/static/images/btn_88x31_built.png"
created "MyApp/root/static/images/btn_88x31_built_shadow.png"
created "MyApp/root/static/images/btn_88x31_powered.png"
created "MyApp/root/static/images/btn_88x31_powered_shadow.png"
created "MyApp/root/favicon.ico"
created "MyApp/Makefile.PL"
created "MyApp/script/myapp_cgi.pl"
created "MyApp/script/myapp_fastcgi.pl"
created "MyApp/script/myapp_server.pl"
created "MyApp/script/myapp_test.pl"
created "MyApp/script/myapp_create.pl"
```

We'll discuss in detail what each of these files do as we progress through the book, but for now, let's just change to the newly-created `MyApp` directory (`cd MyApp`) and run the following:

```
$ perl script/myapp_server.pl
```

This will start up the development web server. You should see some debugging information appear on the console:

```
[debug] Debug messages enabled
[debug] Loaded plugins:
.----------------------------------------------------------------.
| Catalyst::Plugin::ConfigLoader  0.13                           |
```

```
| Catalyst::Plugin::Static::Simple  0.14                                   |
'--------------------------------------------------------------------------'

[debug] Loaded dispatcher "Catalyst::Dispatcher"
[debug] Loaded engine "Catalyst::Engine::HTTP"
[debug] Found home "/home/jon/projects/book/chapter2/MyApp"
[debug] Loaded Config "/home/jon/projects/book/chapter2/MyApp/myapp.yml"
[debug] Loaded components:
.-------------------------------------------------------------+----------.
| Class                                                       | Type   +-
--------------------------------------------------------------+----------+
| MyApp::Controller::Root                                     | instance |
'-----------------------------------------    ----------------+----------'

[debug] Loaded Private actions:
.----------------------+------------  -----------------+-------------.
| Private              | Class                         | Method      |
+----------------------+-------------------------------+-------------+
| /default             | MyApp::Controller::Root       | default     |
| /end                 | MyApp::Controller::Root       | end         |
'----------------------+-------------------------------+-------------'

[info] MyApp powered by Catalyst 5.7010
You can connect to your server at http://localhost:3000
```

This debugging information contains a summary of plug-ins, models, views and controllers that your application uses, in addition to showing a map of URLs to actions. As we haven't added anything to the application as yet, this isn't particularly helpful, but it will become so as we add features.

To see what your application looks like in a browser, simply browse to `http://localhost:3000`.

You should see the standard Catalyst welcome page as follows:

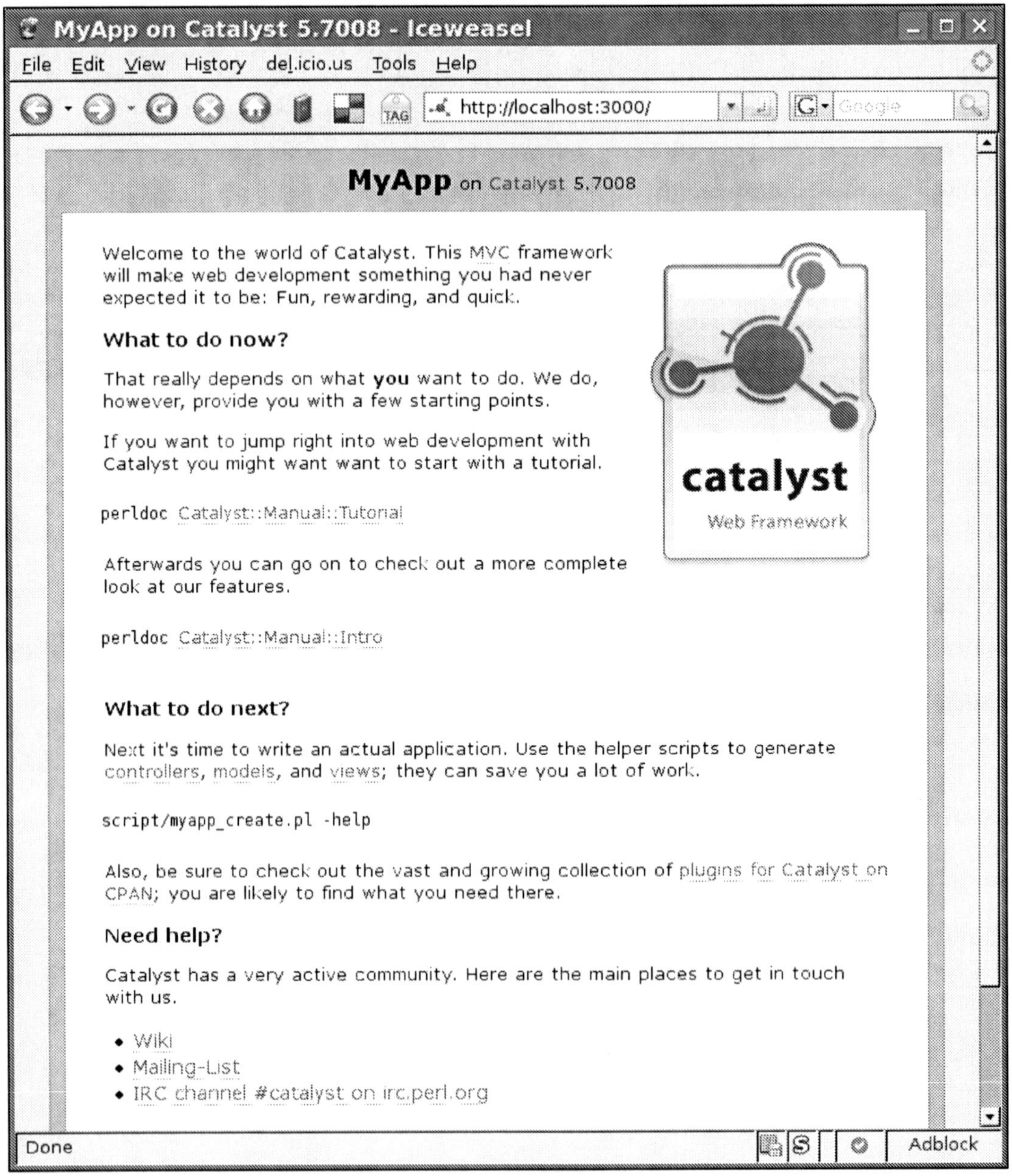

Let's put the application aside for a moment, and see what all the files that were created are used for.

# MyApp Directory Structure

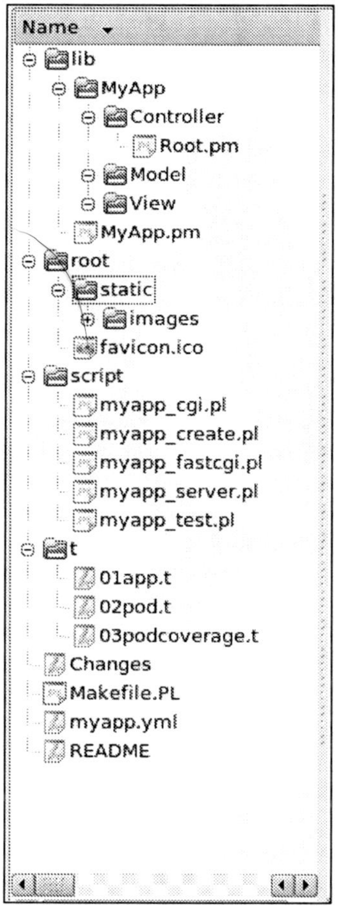


Before we start modifying `MyApp`, let's take a look at how a Catalyst application is structured on a disk. In the root directory of your application, there are some support files. If you're familiar with `CPAN` modules, you'll be at home with Catalyst. A Catalyst application is structured in exactly the same way (and can be uploaded to the `CPAN` unmodified, if desired).

> This chapter will refer to MyApp as your application's name, so if you use something else, be sure to substitute appropriately.

# Files in the MyApp Directory

`Makefile.PL`: This is a script that will generate a makefile to build, test and install your application. It can also contain a list of your application's CPAN dependencies and automatically install them.
To run `Makefile.PL` and generate a `Makefile`, simply type `perl Makefile.PL`. After that, you can run `make` to build the app, `make test` to test the app (you can try this right now, as some sample tests have already been created), `make install` to install the app, and so on. For full details, see the `Module::Install` documentation. It's important that you don't delete this file. Catalyst looks for it to determine where the root of your application is.

`Changes`: This is simply a free-form text file where you can document changes to your application. It's not required, but it can be helpful to end-users or other developers working on your application, especially if you're writing an open-source application.

`README`: This is just a text file with information on your application. If you're not going to distribute your application, you don't need to keep it around.

`myapp.yml`: This is your application's main configuration file, which is loaded when you start your application. You can specify configuration directly inside your application, but this file makes it easier to tweak settings without worrying about breaking your code. `myapp.yml` is in YAML format, but if you rename the file to `myapp.pl`, you can write it in Perl (or `myapp.conf` for Apache-style syntax; see the `Config::Any` manual for a full list).

The name of this file is based on your application's name. Everything is converted to lowercase, double colons are replaced with underscores, and the `yml` extension is appended.

# Files in the lib Directory

- The heart of your application lives in the `lib` directory.
- This directory contains a file called `MyApp.pm`, which is the main file for your application.

This is where you can specify plug-ins to load, as well as the default configuration.

- Inside `lib` are the three key directories, `MyApp/Controller`, `MyApp/Model`, and `MyApp/View`.

  These directories are where your Controllers, Models, and Views will live.

- Right now there's one Controller called `Root.pm`. This will handle all URLs that are in the "root" of your application, and is where the code that generates the welcome page is located.

Keep in mind that "`MyApp`" will be replaced with whatever you passed to `catalyst.pl` when you created the application, and that double colons in the application name will create separate subdirectories on the filesystem. For example, `catalyst.pl MyCompany::HR::Timeslips` would create `lib/MyCompany/HR/Timeslips.pm`, `lib/MyCompany/HR/Timeslips/Controller/`, `mycompany_hr_timeslips.yml`, and other similarly-named files.

# Files in the root Directory

The next special directory is the `root` directory. This directory will hold your templates and other non-code support files. A subdirectory called `/root/static` is for static content like images and style sheets. Catalyst is set up to serve static files from this directory automatically (under the "`/static`" path).

# Files in the script Directory

Finally, there is the `script` directory that contains the scripts needed to run and modify your application.

`myapp_server.pl` is the development server; a self-contained HTTP server that you can use to see your application while you're developing it.

`myapp_cgi.pl` is a CGI script for deploying your application with a web server that cannot use **mod_perl** or **FastCGI**. It's very slow, so use it only as a last resort.

The last server is called `myapp_fastcgi.pl`, which allows you to run your application as a FastCGI server. In Chapter 9, we'll see how to use these scripts to run our application in a production environment.

There are also two utility scripts in this directory. You can use the `myapp_test.pl` script to test an action, without opening a web browser. For example, you can print the source of the welcome page by running the following command line:

```
$ perl script/myapp_test.pl /
```

The last script is `myapp_create.pl`, which is a version of `catalyst.pl` that's customized for your application. It can create models, views, controllers, tests and many other things. We'll use it in the next two sections to create a View and Model for `MyApp`.

All of the scripts in the `script` directory accept command-line arguments to customize their behavior. `perl script/myapp_<scriptname>.pl --help` will explain the details for a specific script.

# Files in the t Directory

The `t` directory is where your application's automatic tests are stored. By default, you'll have three tests as given below:

1. `01app.t`, which is a test that passes if your application compiles.
2. `02pod.t`, which will pass if your POD (*Plain Old Documentation*; embedded API documentation inside your application) is valid.
3. `03podcoverage.t`, which tests that every public function in your application has some documentation.

You can run the tests in this command by running `make test`, after `Makefile.PL` creates the `Makefile`.

# Adding a View

To begin customizing our application, let's start by adding a View that allows us to use the **Template Toolkit** to render HTML pages. The View is a component which is called after your action runs to convert the data that your action put in the **stash** into HTML (or another format suitable for the end user; JSON and XML are also commonly used).

The Template Toolkit is included with the `Catalyst::Devel` package, so you should already have it. You'll need to install the Catalyst interface to it though, by running the following command line:

```
$ cpan -i Catalyst::View::TT
```

If you don't have TT for some reason, `cpan` will detect that and install it for you.

Once that's complete, create the View by running the following command line:

```
$ perl script/myapp_create.pl view TT TT
```

The "`TT TT`" part of the above command means create a view called `View/TT.pm` (the first `TT`) based on the standard `Catalyst::View::TT` (the second `TT`). You can choose any valid Perl filename as the name of your view, but a simple "`TT`" makes the most sense here.

Next, it's a good idea to add `Catalyst::View::TT` to the prerequisites section of `Makefile.PL`. Your application will run fine if you omit this step, but if you're diligent about adding your prerequisites to `Makefile.PL`, it will be very easy to move your application to another machine. A simple `perl Makefile.PL && make` on the new machine will allow Catalyst to automatically install all of your application's dependencies while you have a cup of coffee and relax. A minute of your time here will save much more time later.

Currently, the `Makefile.PL` looks something like the following:

```
use inc::Module::Install;
name 'MyApp';
all_from 'lib/MyApp.pm';
requires 'Catalyst' => '5.7005';
requires 'Catalyst::Plugin::ConfigLoader';
requires 'Catalyst::Plugin::Static::Simple';
requires 'Catalyst::Action::RenderView';
requires 'YAML'; # This should reflect the config file format you've
                 # chosen
            # See Catalyst::Plugin::ConfigLoader for supported formats
catalyst();
install_script glob('script/*.pl');
auto_install();
catalyst_par();
WriteAll();
```

All you need to do to add a prerequisite, is add a line like:

```
requires 'Catalyst::View::TT' => 0;
```

near the other require statements above (order isn't important). The `0` represents the minimum version of the module that your application requires. Leaving it at `0` is fine if you don't know the version, but it's best to specify the current version you're using to develop with. You can determine the version of any module on your system by typing `perl -MSome::Module -e 'print Some::Module->VERSION'`.

The next step is to create a template in `root` directory. For this example, we're going to make a page that says "Hello, world!", so let's call it `hello.tt`.

Here's the code:

```
<?xml version="1.0" encoding="utf-8"?>
<!DOCTYPE html PUBLIC "-//W3C//DTD XHTML 1.1//EN"
          "http://www.w3.org/TR/xhtml11/DTD/xhtml11.dtd">
          "http://www.w3.org/TR/xhtml11/DTD/xhtml11.dtd">
<html xmlns=" http://www.w3.org/1999/xhtml" xml:lang="en">
  <head>
    <title>Hello, world!</title>
  </head>
  <body>
    <h1>Hello, world.</h1>
    <p>
      Here's a word from our Controller:
      [% word | html %].
    </p>
  </body>
</html>
```

This is just a regular XHTML file, with some special control sequences for the Template Toolkit. `[% word%]` tells TT to get a variable called "word" and print it at that point in the template. The `| html` part after "`word`" in the example above is a TT filter that means to escape any HTML in `word` so that `<` is rendered as an actual `<` sign and not an HTML tag. This prevents a type of security hole called "XSS" (cross-site scripting). While security probably isn't important for a "hello world" page, it's wise to get into good habits now.

Right now, this `hello.tt` doesn't do anything, because we haven't told our application to use the TT view yet. Let's create a new controller called "Hello" to manage this page (and make it available at `/hello`):

**`perl script/myapp_create.pl controller Hello`**

This will create `/lib/MyApp/Controller/Hello.pm` (and `/t/controller_hello.t`, which we won't use until Chapter 8):

```
package MyApp::Controller::Hello;
use strict;
use warnings;
use base 'Catalyst::Controller';
=head1 NAME
MyApp::Controller::Hello - Catalyst Controller
=head1 DESCRIPTION
Catalyst Controller.
=head1 METHODS
```

```
=cut

=head2 index

=cut

sub index : Private {
    my ( $self, $c ) = @_;
    $c->response->body('Matched MyApp::Controller::Hello in Hello.');
}

=head1 AUTHOR

Your Name

=head1 LICENSE

This library is free software; you can redistribute it and/or
modify it under the same terms as Perl itself.

=cut

1;
```

This file consists of three parts. Up at the top is a package declaration (so Perl knows what this module is named), and then some use statements (to tell Perl that this module is a Catalyst controller). Next, there is some **POD** that you can fill in to provide some API documentation. (See `man perlpod` for the syntax.) If you don't think you need documentation, you can delete it; it's ignored by Perl. The `perldoc` utility included with `perl` will process this documentation into text, HTML, LaTeX, etc.

Next there's an `index` subroutine. Following that is some more documentation and a `1`. The `1` is important to Perl for historical reasons and must not be removed. (Modules must return true when they're loaded, otherwise Perl will assume that the loading has failed and will die with an error message. `1` is always true, so it's conventional to use it for this purpose.)

The `index` subroutine (actually an Action, as it has an attribute after it) is what we want to modify. As the name suggests, `index` will be run when a directory index for `/hello` is requested. The URL `/hello` is derived from the name of the controller with colons converted to / and the "Hello" from `Hello.pm` converted to all lower case. The `:Private` attribute after `index` tells Catalyst to handle the `index` action internally using special rules. If we specified `:Local` instead of `:Private`, then Catalyst would map the `index` Action to handle a URL that looks like `/hello/index`, which is not quite what we want. (If we omitted the attribute, Catalyst would ignore the action entirely.)

Note that throughout the book instead of a generic `index` action, we will use code like the following:

```
sub list_everything :Path Args(0) { ... }
```

This syntax is more explicit and works with *Chained*, an advanced feature we'll see in Chapter 5.

As we want to be able to handle more than just an `index`, we need to rename the subroutine. Let's call it `hello :Global`. This will allow the `hello` action to handle everything under `/hello`, instead of just `/hello/`. This will allow us to supply an argument (the word to print in `[% word %]`) directly in the URL. (This `hello` action could also have been implemented in `Root.pm` as a `:Local` action, but implementing it in its own file makes it easier to edit without affecting other parts of the application.)

After we make that change, we also need to change the first line of the hello subroutine. Right now, it looks like `my ( $self, $c ) = @_;`. This gets the first two arguments passed to the Action by Catalyst, `$self`, and `$c`. `$self` is a `MyApp::Controller::Hello` object, and is not of much use right now. `$c` is the Catalyst context and contains all the information about our application and the current request (and hence is very useful). Catalyst passes more than just `$self` and `$c`, though, so we want to modify that line to read `my ($self, $c, @args)=@_;`. This will allow us to access the rest of the arguments via the `@args` array.

Arguments are everything in the URL that Catalyst didn't use when matching an action. As an example, `/hello/foo/bar` would put `foo` and `bar` in `$args[0]` and `$args[1]`, respectively, and then call the action matching `/hello`.

Next, let's test the application and make sure everything works so far. Save `Hello.pm` and then run `perl script/myapp_test.pl /hello/test`. If everything is correct, `myapp_test.pl` will print out some debugging information and then print "**Matched MyApp::Controller::Hello in Hello**" to the browser. If something else happens, make sure that you typed in your code correctly (a final listing to check against what appears at the end of this section). The `: Global` part is especially important, so be sure that the debugging output mentions it.

```
[debug] Loaded Private actions:
.----------------------+-----------------------------------+-------------.
| Private              | Class                             | Method      |
+----------------------+-----------------------------------+-------------+
| /hello/hello         | MyApp::Controller::Hello          | hello       |
'----------------------+-----------------------------------+-------------'
[debug] Loaded Path actions:
.------------------------------------+-------------------------------------.
| Path                               | Private                             |
+------------------------------------+-------------------------------------+
| /hello                             | /hello/hello                        |
'------------------------------------+-------------------------------------'
```

This will show you that the URL /hello is handled by the private action called /hello/hello and that /hello/hello is the hello subroutine inside MyApp::Controller::Hello.

Once everything is working, we're ready to add the templating code to the hello subroutine.

## Using a Template To Render the Page

We want to replace the $c->response->body('Matched MyApp::Controller::Hello in Hello'); line with the following code:

```
my $word = $args[0] || 'Default word';
$c->stash->{template} = 'hello.tt';
$c->stash->{word}     = $word;
```

The first line assigns the first argument to a variable called word (or uses Default Word if there isn't a first argument). The next line tells the TT view to use hello.tt as the template for rendering this request. Finally, we put $word in the stash as word, so the [% word %] statement in our template can access that variable.

The *stash* is a data structure that exists throughout a single Catalyst request. Data you insert into the stash in an Action will be available to the View (and other Actions). Templates can only access variables that have been explicitly placed here, so it's important to remember to put your useful data in the stash (otherwise it will be gone at the end of the subroutine, instead of the end of the request).

After you've made these changes, your hello subroutine should look like this (and the default index subroutine should be gone):

```
sub hello : Global {
    my ( $self, $c, @args ) = @_;
    my $word = $args[0] || 'Default word';
    $c->stash->{template} = 'hello.tt';
    $c->stash->{word}     = $word;
}
```

With the code setup, you should be ready to view your web page. Open your web browser, start the development server, and surf to http://localhost:3000/hello/test.

You should see your template rendered in the browser.

Changing the `/test` part of the URL should change the word that shows up in the template.

Congratulations, you've created your first dynamic Catalyst application!

If you're interested in experimenting some more with this setup, here are some things to try. Edit the `hello.tt` template to change the look of the page. You shouldn't even need to restart your development server for changes to take effect. After that, add another page to your application by creating another subroutine in `Hello.pm` and another template. Editing `Hello.pm` will require a restart, but you can make the server automatically restart when necessary by running the server like `perl script/myapp_server.pl -r -d`. The `-r` will cause the server to restart when appropriate, and the `-d` will show debugging information, even if you've turned it off inside your application.

# Some Technical Details

At this point, you may be wondering why the `hello.tt` template showed up without your code ever calling any methods in the Template Toolkit View. This is because, the `end` action in the default `Root.pm` uses an **ActionClass** called "**RenderView**". The `end` action in Root is called at the end of every request, and the `RenderView ActionClass` will automatically forward to the default View. If you'd rather be explicit about invoking the view, you can add a line like:

```
$c->forward('View::TT');
```

at the end of your action. (And `RenderView` will stay out of the way.)

If you have more than one view, you should always explicitly forward, since there's not currently a rigorous definition of "default". You can make every action in a single controller forward to the same view by overriding the `end` action in that controller:

```
sub end : Private {
   my ($self, $c) = @_;
   $c->forward('View::TT');$c->forward('View::TT');
}
```

If you override `end` like this, the default `end` in `Root.pm` will not be called. (Only one `end` action is executed per request; the one that's "closest" to the action that started the request cycle.)

`End` actions (as well as the similar `begin` and `auto` actions) will be covered in more detail throughout the book.

# Adding a Database

The other component that many web applications require is a SQL relational database. Catalyst supports many ways of accessing databases, but the most popular is via an **Object-Relational Mapper** (ORM) called **DBIx::Class** (DBIC). Object-relational mappers allow you to perform operations on your database as though each database object were a Perl object. This means that instead of writing SQL like `SELECT * FROM table`, you can instead say `@results = $table->all`. The advantage of this approach is that DBIC handles the SQL for you, so you can switch from **SQLite** to **DB2** without modifying any of your code. The resulting code in your Controller is also more readable; everything looks like manipulation of Perl data structures. We'll see the power of this approach throughout the book, but for now, let's just create a simple DBIC Model.

You can use any database that you like for this, but I recommend SQLite for development. SQLite is an "embedded" database, so the database exists as a single file and requires no server to run.

# Installing SQLite

The first step is to install SQLite from the SQLite website at `http://sqlite.org/` (or through your distribution's package manager; the package is usually called "sqlite3"). You'll also need to install the Perl version of SQLite, called **DBD::SQLite**, and DBIx::Class itself:

```
$ cpan -i DBD::SQLite DBIx::Class Catalyst::Model::DBIC::Schema
```

# Creating a Database Schema

Once the dependencies are installed, we'll create a sample database with the `sqlite3` command-line utility:

```
$ sqlite3 /tmp/database
SQLite version 3.3.8
Enter ".help" for instructions
sqlite> CREATE TABLE test (id INTEGER PRIMARY KEY, subject TEXT, message
TEXT, date DATETIME);
sqlite> INSERT INTO test (id, subject, message, date) VALUES(NULL, "test
message", "this is a test message", "2005-01-01 00:00");
sqlite> INSERT INTO test (id, subject, message, date) VALUES(NULL,
"another test message", "this is a another test message, hooray", "2005-
01-01 00:01");
sqlite> SELECT * FROM test;
1|test message|this is a test message|2005-01-01 00:00
2|another test message|this is a another test message, hooray|2005-01-01
00:01
sqlite> .quit
$
```

Here we created a "test" table in a database file called `/tmp/database` and added two rows to it.

> SQLite has unusual semantics for auto-incrementing primary keys. You must declare the auto-increment column exactly as "INTEGER PRIMARY KEY" and then assign NULL during INSERT operations. DBIC will handle this automatically, but you should be aware of this unconventional approach when interacting with the database from within the `sqlite3` utility.

# Creating a Database Model for Catalyst

To use this database from Catalyst, we need to create a Catalyst Model. We can do this using the following command line:

```
$ perl script/myapp_create.pl model TestDatabase DBIC::Schema \ MyApp::
Schema::TestDatabase create=dynamic \ dbi:SQLite:/tmp/database
```

The first argument is the name of the Catalyst Model (`TestDatabase`). `DBIC::Schema` is what sort of model we're creating. `MyApp::Schema::TestDatabase` is where the schema definition will be stored (we won't use the **Schema** in this example, but real applications will). `create=dynamic` tells DBIC to read the database every time the application is started to determine the schema (layout of tables, foreign key relations, etc.). The final argument is the *DBI* connect string for the database.

We'll also create another Controller for the database page, to avoid cluttering up the *Hello* or *Root* controllers.

```
$ perl script/myapp_create.pl controller Database
```

Once we have this, we'll create a template to show data from the database in a file called `root/list_messages.tt`. It should look like the following:

```
<?xml version="1.0" encoding="utf-8"?>
<!DOCTYPE html PUBLIC "-//W3C//DTD XHTML 1.1//EN"
                      "http://www.w3.org/TR/xhtml11/DTD/xhtml11.dtd">
<html xmlns="http://www.w3.org/1999/xhtml"
      xml:lang="en">
  <head>
    <title>Hello, database!</title>
  </head>
  <body>
    <h1>Database</h1>
    <p>Here's what the database looks like: </p>
    <ol>
     [% WHILE (message = messages.next) %]
      <li>
         <p>Message <b>[% message.subject | html %]</b>
         (#[% message.id | html %]):</p>
         <p>[% message.message | html %]</p>
         <p>Written at <i>[% message.date | html %]</i>.</p>
      </li>
     [% END %]
    </ol>
  </body>
</html>
```

# Using the Model

Now, we'll want to create code to show this template in the `Database.pm` Controller. In this case, using the `index` action that's automatically generated will be fine, since we don't need any arguments.

We will need to populate a variable called `messages` with the data from our database. The code to do this looks like the following:

```
sub list_messages :Path Args(0) { # same as index :Private
    my ( $self, $c ) = @_;
    $c->stash->{template} = 'list_messages.tt';
    $c->stash->{messages} = $c->model('TestDatabase::test');
}
```

This is almost the same as our hello action, but in this case we fill the `messages` variable with the entires in the `test` table (in the `TestDatabase` Model). The `$c->model(...)` syntax allows you to access any Model by name. DBIC::Schema supports extra syntax to allow you to name a table in the database directly (the `::test` part), so we use that to create a **ResultSet** object.

Once we have the template and results from the database query in the stash, our template takes over. The `[% WHILE (message = messages.next) %]` command loops over each row in the `test` table, and creates a variable called `message` that holds that row. The other `[% ... %]` commands in the template simply extract the data from the row via the column name. That's all there is to it—Catalyst handles the hard stuff for you!

To view your database as an HTML page, start the development server again and browse to `http://localhost:3000/database`.

# Summary

In this chapter, we created our first Catalyst application with the `catalyst.pl` utility. After running the skeleton application and inspecting it with a web browser, we added an HTML template View with the `myapp_create.pl` script and created a "Hello" Controller to display a "Hello, world" page. Finally, we added a database Model using `DBIC::Schema` and created a Controller containing actions that show data from the database, via the View and templates, as an HTML page.

# 3
# Building a Real Application

In this chapter, we're going to build our first real application, an address book. We'll start with a skeleton similar to the application from the last chapter, but then we'll add some real logic to create a **CRUD** (create, retrieve, update, delete) interface to a database.

We'll also learn how to define forms that automatically generate and validate themselves, and how to design a database schema. We'll also use a View that generates common pages for us, so we won't have to worry about style sheets or tricky HTML for now.

# Environment Setup

Before we start writing our new application, we'll need to create a skeleton again. We can create it using the following command lines:

```
$ catalyst.pl AddressBook
$ cd AddressBook/
```

We'll also need two more CPAN modules for this chapter. These can be created using the following:

```
$ cpan Catalyst::Controller::FormBuilder Catalyst::Controller::BindLex
```

The above command will ensure that the latest version of each modules is installed on your system.

After installing the modules, we'll add a special Template Toolkit View called `TTSite` to our application, using the following command line:

```
$ perl script/addressbook_create.pl view HTML TTSite
```

`TTSite` will automatically generate some basic HTML for us, so our templates will only need to contain the text and markup that applies specifically to them. The header, footer, messages and stylesheets will all be handled automatically and will be easy to customize later.

# Database Design

The first real step will be to think about what kind of data we need to store and then design a database schema to efficiently store that data. To keep things simple (but realistic), let's set our specification as follows:

- The address book should keep track of multiple addresses for a person.
- Each person can have a first and last name.
- Each address can have a street address, a phone number and an email address.

Translated into a relational database schema, that means we'll have a "people" table that will assign a unique identifier to each first name and last name pair.

Then we'll have an "addresses" table that will allow each person to have multiple addresses; each consisting of a unique ID (so it's easy to reference later), a location ("Office", "Home"), a free-form postal address (so we don't have to worry about the complexity of having a City, Country, State, Postal Code, etc.), a phone number and an email address. Each row will have a column called "person", which will be the ID of the person that "owns" this address (called a **foreign key** in SQL parlance). We'll also make each field in the addresses table optional (except for the location), so we can have locations like "Mobile" for storing a mobile phone number (without a postal address or email).

Now we just have to express this as SQL, and type it into SQLite as follows:

```
$ sqlite3 database
sqlite> CREATE TABLE people (id INTEGER NOT NULL PRIMARY KEY, firstname
VARCHAR(50) NOT NULL, lastname VARCHAR(50) NOT NULL);
sqlite> CREATE TABLE addresses (id INTEGER NOT NULL PRIMARY KEY, person
INTEGER NOT NULL, location VARCHAR(20), postal TEXT, phone VARCHAR(20),
email VARCHAR(100));
```

Let's also add some sample data, so we can create a "view" page and actually see some data show up as follows:

```
sqlite> INSERT INTO people VALUES(NULL, 'Your', 'Name');
sqlite> INSERT INTO addresses VALUES(NULL, 1, 'Home', '123 Green St.',
'123-456-7890', 'home@example.com');
sqlite> INSERT INTO addresses VALUES(NULL, 1, 'Work', '42 Work St.',
'987-654-3210', 'work@example.com');
sqlite> .quit
```

With the schema configured, let's link the database to a Catalyst model using the following command line:

```
$ perl script/addressbook_create.pl model AddressDB DBIC::Schema
AddressBook::Schema::AddressDB create=static dbi:SQLite:database
```

This will create a Model called `AddressDB`, and it will also create a `Schema/AddressDB` subdirectory that contains the definition of our database schema in `DBIx::Class's` (DBIC) format. This schema will be pre-populated with the schema we just created with the `sqlite3` utility. Keeping the schema in this format will allow us to deploy to any database system that `DBIx::Class` supports by simply running the deploy function in your schema. It will also let us explicitly specify any relations between the tables, so that we can access the data from inside our program in a natural way. This will also allow functionality, like automatically deleting a person's addresses when we delete that person.

# Understanding the Interface to the Database

The exact files generated (inside `lib/AddressBook`) are:

- `Model/AddressDB.pm`

  The actual Model that Catalyst uses. It's simply a stub that points `DBIx::Class` at the `Schema/AddressDB.pm` schema.

- `Schema/AddressDB.pm`

  This is the schema that the Model points to. This is another stub that automatically loads everything in the subdirectory/AddressDB

- `Schema/AddressDB/People.pm` and `Schema/AddressDB/Addresses.pm`

  This is where the real schema data is stored. Each of these files will declare a table name (so that Perl knows that `People.pm` is the `people` table in the database) and the column definitions. Relationships between tables are added here, as are any specific access methods you'd like to add. Accessing a column's data by name is available by default, so most people won't need to add their own methods.

We'll need to dig inside these schema files so that we can specify the relations. Let's look at `People.pm` first.

```
package AddressBook::Schema::AddressDB::People;
use strict;
use warnings;
use base 'DBIx::Class';
__PACKAGE__->load_components("PK::Auto", "Core");
__PACKAGE__->table("people");
__PACKAGE__->add_columns(
  "id",
  { data_type => "INTEGER", is_nullable => 0, size => undef },
  "firstname",
  { data_type => "VARCHAR", is_nullable => 0, size => 50 },
  "lastname",
  { data_type => "VARCHAR", is_nullable => 0, size => 50 },
);
__PACKAGE__->set_primary_key("id");
1;
```

Everything is fairly understandable by default. The module starts like any other (with a package declaration based on the filename, and `use strict` and `use warnings`). We then load `DBIx::Class`. After that, we start configuring the table. First, we load some DBIC components, `core` for the main functionality, and `PK::Auto` to get auto-incrementing primary keys. Next, we tell `DBIx::Class` that this module represents the `people` table in the database. After that, we declare all the columns in the database. The format is simply pairs of column names and their definitions. Lastly, we tell `DBIx::Class` which column is the primary key, so that it can manage relations for us in an intelligent manner.

We do need to add one line to the bottom of the file manually. As every entry in this table can have zero or more addresses (entries in the addresses table) associated with it, it would be useful to access these addresses as though they were data stored in a column (like the "firstname"). In SQL, this is called a "has many" relationship and we use the `has_many` function to make `DBIx::Class` aware of this relationship.

```
__PACKAGE__->has_many(
    addresses => 'AddressBook::Schema::AddressDB::Addresses',
    'person',
    {cascading_delete => 1}  );
```

This looks pretty complicated but it's just a matter of reading everything right. The above example is read as, "This *package* (module, table) **has many** *addresses* in the `AddressBook::Schema::AddressDB::Addresses` table". The column that relates addresses to this package is `person` in the addresses table. `{cascading_delete => 1}` is a configuration option that causes any addresses associated with a person to be deleted when that person is deleted. The name `addresses` we chose above is the name we'll use to access the related data when we have a `person` object around. It can be anything you want; it need not bear any resemblance to a column name in either of the affected tables.

We'll also add one method to this class. It is given as follows:

```
sub name {
    my $self = shift;
    return $self->firstname. ' '. $self->lastname;
}
```

This will allow us to access the full name of the person by simply calling `name` on an instance (much easier that concatenating the `firstname` and `lastname` every time we want to display them together).

Once that's set, we need to do the same things for the auto-generated `Addresses.pm`. The code for this file looks pretty much the same as the `People.pm` file. It is given as follows:

```
package AddressBook::Schema::AddressDB::Addresses;

use strict;
use warnings;

use base 'DBIx::Class';

__PACKAGE__->load_components("PK::Auto", "Core");
__PACKAGE__->table("addresses");
__PACKAGE__->add_columns(
  "id",
  { data_type => "INTEGER", is_nullable => 0, size => undef },
  "person",
  { data_type => "INTEGER", is_nullable => 0, size => undef },
  "location",
  { data_type => "VARCHAR", is_nullable => 1, size => 20 },
  "postal",
  { data_type => "TEXT", is_nullable => 1, size => undef },
  "phone",
  { data_type => "VARCHAR", is_nullable => 1, size => 20 },
  "email",
  { data_type => "VARCHAR", is_nullable => 1, size => 100 },
);
__PACKAGE__->set_primary_key("id");
```

The only modification we need to make is to define a relation from addresses to people. This relation is called `belongs-to` relation and looks like the following:

```
__PACKAGE__->belongs_to(

        person => 'AddressBook::Schema::AddressDB::People');
```

This simply says that the `person` column in this table is a foreign key into the `AddressBook::Schema::AddressDB::People` table. In terms of coding, this means that when we access `$some_address->person` we will get the Person object that this address is associated with instead of the database's ID number for that person.

That's all we need to do with the Model for this section. Let us put this aside for a moment and turn our focus to the View.

# TTSite

`TTSite` is a Catalyst View that wraps every TT template we use in a header and footer. This all happens transparently, so we can add some prettiness to our site without writing any CSS or HTML.

There are a few differences from the standard TT view to be aware of. First, templates are stored in `/root/src` instead of `/root`. TTSite keeps its configuration in `/root/lib`, so that's where you'll want to go if you want to change the look of the site. The configuration is easy to understand—the file called `header` contains the TT commands that will be added to the header of the page (and so on).

For this application, we do need to make a few modifications to the default setup. First, let's remove the default "message" (to display at the top of the page), so we can specify our own from a controller.

To do this, edit `/root/lib/config/main`, removing the block of code that looks like this:

```
# set defaults for variables, etc.
DEFAULT
  message = 'There is no message';
```

Next, we'll edit the template that formats our main content so that it will show us a `message` if it exists (and an `error` message if one exists). In `/root/lib/site/layout`, add the following lines after the `<div id="content">` and before the `[% content %]` command:

```
[% IF error %]
  <p><span class="error">[% error | html %]</span></p>
[% END %]
[% IF message %]
  <p><span class="message">[% message | html %]</span></p>
[% END %]
```

This change will allow our controllers to set messages (or error) that will display above the content. This means we can skip the step of adding error screens or success screens. For example, after adding an address, we can return the user to the list of addresses and add a message saying *Address added successfully!*. This is in contrast to the traditional scheme of having an entire page with the message and a link to *go back*.

Finally, we need to edit `/lib/AddressBook/View/HTML.pm` and add a line to set the default template extension to `.tt2`. Simply add the following:

```
TEMPLATE_EXTENSION  => '.tt2',
```

before the `TIMER => 0` line. This will cause Catalyst to automatically pick which template to render based on the name of the action. For example, the action `/person/edit` will automatically use the template in `root/src/person/edit.tt2`, which will save us some typing later on.

That's all we need to get a comfortable View set up, so let's start adding some pages!

# Creating the Index Page

The first pages we need to add are an index page and a "not found" page. The index page goes in `/root/src/index.tt2`, and looks like the following:

```
[% META title = "Welcome to the Address Book" %]
<p>Here you will find All Things Address.</p>
<p>From here, you can:
<ul>
<li><a href="[% Catalyst.uri_for('/person/list') %]">Look at all
people</a></li>
<li><a href="[% Catalyst.uri_for('/person/add') %]">Add a new person</
a></li>
</ul>
</p>
```

As you can see, `TTSite` saved us a bit of work here. All we have to do is set the title, and then provide the content. In this case, we're just printing out two links, one to list all people and another to add a new person. Note that instead of specifying URLs directly, we use `Catalyst.uri_for` and then the internal name of the action (displayed in the debugging output). This ensures that the URL that's generated will always be correct, even if your application is moved to a different host or subdirectory, or, if you change your action from `Local` to `Global`, or something similar.

# Creating a "Not Found" Page

Next, we need a "not found" page to show to the user when they enter an invalid URL. We'll call this `not_found.tt2` and it will live in the same directory as `index.tt2`:

```
[% META title = '404 Not Found' %]
<p>We couldn't find the page you were looking for.
Maybe you'd like to
<a href="[% Catalyst.uri_for('/') %]">go home</a> instead?
</p>
```

Now that we have the templates, we need to add some actions in the Root controller that will show them when appropriate. The code in /lib/AddressBook/Controller/Root.pm should look like this (replacing the auto-generated default and index actions, but nothing else):

```
sub default : Private {
    my ( $self, $c ) = @_;
    $c->response->status('404');
    $c->stash->{template} = 'not_found.tt2';
}
sub index : Private {};
```

This is the same thing that we did in the last chapter, except in the index action we don't need to do anything, since TTSite will automatically render index.tt2 when the index action is called.

With that, we're ready to take a first look at our application. Start up the development server using the following command line:

```
$ perl script/addressbook_server.pl -r -d
```

Then navigate to http://localhost:3000/. The index page should show up like the following:

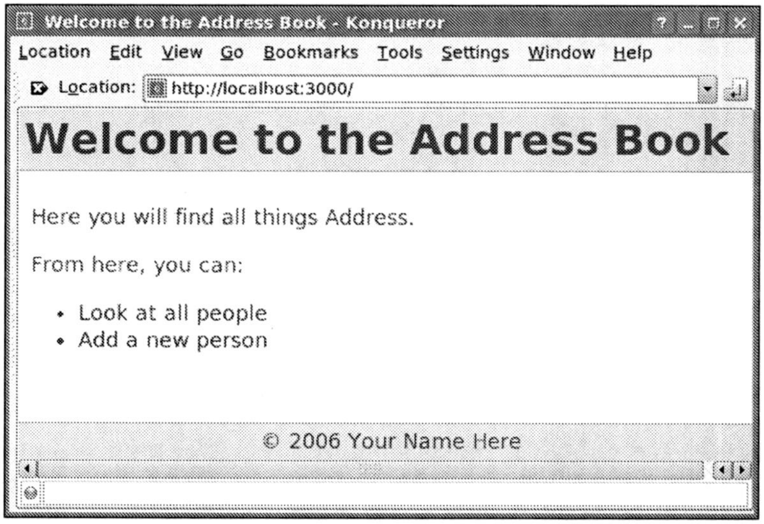


Then navigate to http://localhost:3000/this/does/not/exist. You should see the error page and be able to click a link to get back to the index page.

If that works, we're ready to start writing the real code!

# Viewing People

The first link on the index page is **Look at all people**, so let's create an action that will display everyone in our database, along with their addresses (if any). We'll also show links to relevant actions such as "edit name", "add address" and "delete person". The eventual goal is to have a page that looks something like this:

The page is a little busy, but it conveys all the information that we want to. (You'll also note that Catalyst and Perl can handle Unicode data flawlessly.)

The first thing we need to do is to create a People controller for managing people. This controller will have add, delete and list actions for each person. (The list action actually shows every person, which is convenient even if the grammar isn't perfect.)

We'll be deviating a bit from the standard template controller, so there's no reason to automatically generate one. Let's just start with this code, inside `lib/AddressBook/Controller/Person.pm`:

```
package AddressBook::Controller::Person;
use strict;
use warnings;
use base 'Catalyst::Controller::BindLex';
sub list : Local {
    my ($self, $c) = @_;
    my $people : Stashed = $c->model('AddressDB::People');
    $c->stash->{template} = 'person/list.tt2';
}
1;
```

This controller is slightly different from the one we used in the last chapter. Instead of using `Catalyst::Controller` as our base class, we're using `Catalyst::Controller::BindLex`. `BindLex` works just like a regular controller, but it gives you the ability to add `: Stashed` after any variable name to automatically store it in the stash. This will save us typing when we need to use a value in both the controller and in the template. Without `BindLex`, you would use the variable normally in the controller and then manually save it in `$c->stash` in order to see the value inside the template.

After that, we add a Local `list` action that gets all the People out of the database and stores them in `$people` (and `$c->stash->{people}`). Finally, we set the template to `person/list.tt2`, and we're done. (Note that although this action would use that template by default, we specify it explicitly so that other actions that forward to this page will also display the `list.tt2` template.)

That's all the controller needs to do to create a page like the one in the above screenshot. Now, we just need the `list.tt2` template, inside `root/src/person/list.tt2`:

```
[% META title = 'People' %]

[% IF people.count > 0 %]
<p>Here are people that I know about:</p>
<ul>
[% WHILE (person = people.next) %]
<li>
  [% person.name | html %]
  <a href="[% Catalyst.uri_for("/address/add/$person.id") | html
%]">Add address</a>
  <a href="[% Catalyst.uri_for("/person/edit/$person.id") | html
%]">Edit</a>
  <a href="[% Catalyst.uri_for("/person/delete/$person.id") | html
%]">Delete</a>
```

```
    [% SET addresses = person.addresses %]
    <ul>
    [% FOREACH address = addresses %]
     <li>
     <b>[% address.location | html  %]</b>
      <a href="[% Catalyst.uri_for("/address/edit/$address.id") | html
%]">
      Edit</a>
      <a href="[% Catalyst.uri_for("/address/delete/$address.id") | html
%]">
      Delete</a>
      <br />
      <address>
        [% address.postal | html | html_line_break %]
      </address>
      Phone: [% address.phone | html %]<br />
      Email: [% address.email | html %]<br />
     </li>
    [% END %]
    </ul>
  </li>
  [% END %]
  </ul>
  [% ELSE %]
  <p>No people yet!</p>
  [% END %]
  <p><a href="[% Catalyst.uri_for("/person/add") | html %]">
    Add a new person...
  </a></p>
```

This looks fairly complex, but it's mostly HTML that makes the data from the database look nice. The bulk of the code consists of a `WHILE` loop that iterates over each Person in the database. Once we have a `Person` object, we can print out the first name, last name and some links to pages where we can edit and delete people and addresses (we'll create these pages later). After that, we get an array of Addresses associated with this person (from the relationship we added to the schema earlier in the chapter). We iterate over each element in that array and print out the location, postal address, phone number and email address associated for that address. When there are no more addresses, we return to the `WHILE` loop and get the next Person in the database. This continues until everything in the database has been printed.

To see this in action, start up the server, add some new people and addresses to the database (via the sqlite3 utility) and watch them appear on the page at `http://localhost:3000/person/list`.

# Basic CRUD

Let's start by writing the easiest method, a method to delete a person from the database. All we need is a simple action in the Person controller:

```
sub delete : Local {
    my ($self, $c, $id) = @_;
    my $person : Stashed = $c->model('AddressDB::People')->
                                              find({id => $id});
    if($person){
        $c->stash->{message} = 'Deleted '. $person->name;
        $person->delete;
    }
    else {
        $c->stash->{error} = "No person $id";
    }
    $c->forward('list');
}
```

This action will create a URL that looks like `/person/delete/1`, where 1 is the person's ID number in the database. Using that ID number that's passed in the URL, we look for the row in the database with that ID. If we find one, we set the status message to `Deleted Person's Name` and then delete the person. (The delete method will also remove any addresses that were associated with that person.) If there's no person in the database matching that ID, we set an error message instead.

Regardless of the outcome, we forward back to the list page we came from. There, the new data will show up, with an appropriate message at the top of the screen. This makes it very easy for the user to be sure that his action took effect—there's a message saying that it did and the user can look at the list of people and confirm that the person deleted is gone—and it makes it easy to perform another operation, as he doesn't have to navigate anywhere. The only disadvantage is that the URL in the URL bar is no longer correct. For now, we'll live with this, but in the next chapter we'll see how to keep the URL correct and forward the user around in the same way.

# Forms

Now that you've deleted the sample row you added when you created the database, we'll need to implement methods for adding (and editing) a person.

Since creating and validating HTML forms is a repetitive and boring task, we're going to use `Catalyst::controller::FormBuilder` to automatically build our forms. All we have to do is create a definition of the form and `FormBuilder` will generate the HTML and validate it when the user submits it. If there's a problem with one of the fields, `FormBuilder` will return the form to the user with an appropriate message. If the user's browser supports JavaScript, `FormBuilder` will validate the form on the client side to save a round-trip. (The data will be validated again on the server and rejected if it's bad. This prevents users from turning off JavaScript and submitting bad data.)

The first form to add is the "edit name" form. Since the action will be located at '`/person/edit`', the form definition will live in the `/root/forms/person/edit.fb` file. This file contains the following:

```
name: person_edit
method: post
fields:
  firstname:
    label: First Name
    type: text
    size: 30
    required: 1
  lastname:
    label: Last Name
    type: text
    size: 30
    required: 1
```

We'll also need a template where we can render this form, so inside `/root/src/person/edit.tt2`, we'll add a very small template:

```
[% META title = "Edit a person" %]
[% form.render %]
```

This is all we need to generate a form for adding a person or changing a person's name. Before we add all the form logic, let's write a simple action in the Person controller so we can see what the form looks like:

```
sub edit : Local Form {
    my ($self, $c) = @_;

    if ($c->form->submitted && $c->form->validate) {
        $c->stash->{message} = 'Thanks for submitting the form!';
    }
}
```

We also need to inherit from `Catalyst::Controller::FormBuilder` at the top of the Controller file:

```
use base qw(Catalyst::Controller::FormBuilder Catalyst::Controller::
BindLex);
```

This new `use base` line will replace the existing line (which only loads `BindLex`).

You can now start up the development server and navigate to `http://localhost:3000/person/edit`. You should see the form that you defined in the `edit.fb` form definition file. Try entering some text and clicking submit. If your entries are acceptable (according to the constraints specified in the form definition), then `$c->form->validate` will return true and the *Thanks for submitting the form!* message will appear at the top of your page. If you manage to submit some invalid data (one of the names left blank, for example), then `FormBuilder` will return you to the form and mark the fields that have errors in red.

Now that our form works, we just need to add some database logic to have a fully working action. The final action looks like this:

```
sub edit : Local Form {
    my ($self, $c, $id) = @_;
    my $person = $c->model('AddressDB::People')->
                            find_or_new({id => $id});
    if ($c->form->submitted && $c->form->validate) {
        # form was submitted and it validated
        $person->firstname($c->form->field('firstname'));
        $person->lastname ($c->form->field( 'lastname'));
        $person->update_or_insert;
        $c->stash->{message} =
          ($id > 0 ? 'Updated ' : 'Added ') . $person->name;
        $c->forward('list');
    }
    else {
         # first time through, or invalid form
         if(!$id){
           $c->stash->{message} = 'Adding a new person';
         }
         $c->form->field(name  => 'firstname',
                               value => $person->firstname);
         $c->form->field(name  => 'lastname',
                               value => $person->lastname);
    }
}
```

Here's what happens: The action is set up to accept the numeric ID of the person to edit. We use this ID number to view the person with that ID in the database via the `find_or_new` DBIC method. The `find` method by itself will work for locating existing records, but using `find_or_new` instead will create a new record if there's no matching record already in the database. The new record that is created is not actually written to the database; it only exists in memory. Only when we insert the record explicitly will it be created in the database. This allows us to call `find_or_new` each time the action is called because we only `insert_or_update` the record when we've verified that the data is valid. (If we used `find_or_create` instead of `find_or_new`, we'd create a record every time someone requested the form. That would lead to a lot of useless data in the database.)

After we have a record to manipulate, we check whether the form has been submitted (`$c->form->submitted`) and if so, whether the form data is valid according to the `edit.fb` file (`$c->form->validate`). If both of these conditions are true, we transfer the data from the form to the database and then `update_or_insert` the record (insert if the record is new, update if it already exists; DBIC will figure out which one is appropriate). Then, we add a message to the stash, and forward it to the list page (so the user can edit another person and see the new person along with the existing people).

If the form hasn't been submitted yet, or the data's not valid, we transfer the firstname and lastname from the database to the form and let `FormBuilder` display the form (again). Although we transfer the database information to the form each time, the submitted form data will override the database data. This can be prevented by passing the `force => 1` option to `$c->form->field`, in which case the database data will override the form data.

Although the `edit` action actually handles adding new entries, it's a good idea to have a separate `add` action as well. This will allow you to be flexible in the future; if you decide that the add form should be different from the edit form, you can make that change without finding all links to `edit` that actually add. (Make sure that you use `$c->uri_for('/person/add')` instead of `$c->uri_for('/person/edit')` when generating links though. Even though they do the same thing now, they won't if you change the `add` action later.)

Here's the add action that redirects the user to the edit action:

```
sub add : Local {
    my ($self, $c) = @_;
    $c->response->redirect($c->uri_for('edit'));
}
```

If you'd prefer not to do a client-side redirect, you can add code like this instead:

```
sub add : Local Form('/person/edit') {
    my ($self, $c) = @_;
    $c->stash->{template} = 'person/edit.tt2';
    $c->forward('edit', []);
}
```

This makes for a cleaner application, but makes for extra typing to get the same functionality.

The `[]` in the `forward` statement tells Catalyst to throw away any arguments that were passed to the action. This way, visiting the URL `/person/add/2` will add a new person, not edit person #2.

# Finishing Up

The final feature we need to add to our address book is an address editing controller, with methods for adding, editing and deleting addresses. Even though the address data is more complicated than the simple firstname/lastname records that we were working with before, the code is almost exactly the same.

Let's start by creating a template for the address editing form, in `root/src/address/edit.tt2`:

```
[% META title = "Address" %]
<p>Here's some text explaining the form below.  Only the "location"
field is required, etc., etc.</p>
[% form.render %]
```

This looks just like the name editing form. In a real application, you will want to add some text explaining the form so that your users know what constraints are placed on the data. Since this is just another template, you can add as much text before or after the form as you feel is appropriate. You can also use variables from the stash, and so on.

Next, we want to add a definition of the form in `root/forms/address/edit.fb`. This can be done in the following manner:

```
name: address_edit
method: POST
title: Address
fields:
  location:
    label: Location
    type: select
```

```
      options: Home, Office, Mobile
      other: 1
      required: 1
    postal:
      label: Mailing Address
      type: textarea
      rows: 4
      cols: 60
    phone:
      label: Phone Number
      validate: PHONE
    email:
      label: E-Mail Address
      validate: EMAIL
```

In this form, we're taking advantage of some of `FormBuidler's` more advanced features. The first field, location, is declared to be a dropdown menu with "Home", "Office", and "Mobile" as options. We also tell `FormBuilder` to provide an "other" option. This will create a textfield that can be filled out to declare a location other than one of the options we explicitly mentioned. `FormBuilder` will automatically generate the JavaScript required to hide and unhide this field as appropriate.

The `phone` and `email` fields are also special. Since we want to make sure that the user submits realistic phone numbers and email addresses, we tell `FormBuilder` to use its built-in `EMAIL` and `PHONE` validators (see the `FormBuilder` documentation for a full list of validation types). If the built-in validation functions don't meet your needs, you can also specify a regular expression in single quotes instead. `FormBuilder` will generate the JavaScript equivalent of this regex for client-side validation and then use the regex as you specified it for the server-side validation. This is extremely convenient for complicated forms.

With that out of the way, all we need to do is write the controller, `lib/AddressBook/Controller/Address.pm`:

```
package AddressBook::Controller::Address;
use strict;
use warnings;
use base qw(Catalyst::Controller::FormBuilder Catalyst::Controller::
BindLex');
sub add : Local Form('/address/edit') {
    my ($self, $c, $person_id) = @_;
    $c->stash->{template} = 'address/edit.tt2';
    $c->forward('edit', [undef, $person_id]);
}
```

```
sub edit : Local Form {
    my ($self, $c, $address_id, $person_id) = @_;
    my $address : Stashed;
    if(!$address_id && $person_id){
       # we're adding a new address to $person
       # check that person exists
       my $person = $c->model('AddressDB::People')->
                                 find({id => $person_id});
        if(!$person){
           $c->stash->{error} = 'No such person!';
           $c->detach('/person/list');
        }
       # create the new address
        $address = $c->model('AddressDB::Addresses')->
                                new({person => $person});

    }
    else {
       $address = $c->model('AddressDB::Addresses')->
                               find({id => $address_id});
       if(!$address){
          $c->stash->{error} = 'No such address!';
          $c->detach('/person/list');
       }
    }

    if ($c->form->submitted && $c->form->validate){
        # transfer data from form to database
       $address->location($c->form->field('location'));
       $address->postal  ($c->form->field('postal'  ));
       $address->phone   ($c->form->field('phone'   ));
       $address->email   ($c->form->field('email'   ));
       $address->insert_or_update;
       $c->stash->{message} =
          ($address_id > 0 ? 'Updated ' : 'Added new ').
                      'address for '. $address->person->name;
       $c->detach('/person/list');
   }
   else {
      # transfer data from database to form
      if(!$address_id){
         $c->stash->{message} = 'Adding a new address ';
      }
```

```
        else {
            $c->stash->{message} = 'Updating an address ';
        }
        $c->stash->{message} .= ' for '. $address->person->name;
        $c->form->field(name  => 'location',
                        value => $address->location);
        $c->form->field(name  => 'postal',
                        value => $address->postal);
        $c->form->field(name  => 'phone',
                        value => $address->phone);
        $c->form->field(name  => 'email',
                        value => $address->email);
    }
}
sub delete : Local {
    my ($self, $c, $address_id) = @_;
    my $address = $c->model('AddressDB::Addresses')->
                                  find({id => $address_id});
    if($address){
        # "Deleted First Last's Home address"
        $c->stash->{message} =
            'Deleted ' . $address->person->name. q{'s }.
                $address->location. ' address';
        $address->delete;
    }
    else {
        $c->stash->{error} = 'No such address';
    }

    $c->forward('/person/list');
}
1;
```

This controller employs the same techniques as the `Person.pm` controller, but some of the details are different. First, the `edit` action accepts two arguments, the address's ID and the person's ID. This creates a URL like `/address/edit/0/5`. This is so the `edit` action can also create new addresses. When we edit an address, we specify only the address ID. When we want to create an address, we leave the address ID undefined (or zero) and specify the person's ID instead. This is a little unwieldy, so we abstract these details out to the `add` action. The `add` action accepts the person's ID and then forwards the appropriate data to the `edit` action.

Once inside the edit action, we determine whether we're adding or editing. If we're adding, we create a new row in the database that's linked to the person that was passed in. Note that when we create the row, we assign the actual person object to the person column, not the person's ID number. Although the database actually stores the relation from an address to its person via an ID number, this is a detail that DBIC handles for us. We only have to think about what we mean, not how the database represents relations.

If it turns out the person ID that was passed doesn't exist in the database, we return the user to the list of people and addresses with an error message at the top.

If we're instead editing an existing address, we just look up the address by the address ID number that was passed into the action. If we can't find one, we return the user to the list page with an error message.

At this point, we have an address object (existing or newly-created) that we can use to populate the form. The rest of the action looks just like the one for adding or editing a person, except we have a few more fields this time.

The address delete action also works exactly like the person deletion action, except we delete an address object instead of a person object.

Since we already added code to list addresses to the `/person/list` template, we can restart the server, browse to that page (`http://localhost:3000/person/list`) and try adding some addresses. You should now have full creation, listing editing, and deletion facilities, all tied together with a consistent look-and-feel.

# Summary

In this chapter, we created a full **CRUD** application. We started by creating a database schema inside of SQLite. Then we created a Catalyst model for accessing this database. Since SQLite doesn't handle foreign key relations by itself, we added information about the relations between tables directly to the DBIC schema files. Once that was set up, we customized the `TTSite` View and created a page that listed all people and addresses in the database. Then, we created a controller to edit, add and delete people. The edit and add actions were simple forms, so we used `Catalyst::Controller::FormBuilder` to generate and validate the forms automatically. After this controller was built, we created a similar one to add, edit and update addresses, again using `FormBuilder` to generate the form HTML and JavaScript for us.

# 4
# Expanding the Application

In this chapter, we will continue to work with our *address book* application and add some features that almost every application needs. We'll see how to move the configuration options out of application code and into an easy-to-maintain configuration file. We'll also learn how to search a database and create search results that span multiple pages. To bulk up our database so that searching is more meaningful, we'll write a script to import CSV files into the address book. We will also add sessions to our application, so that data can persist between requests. Finally, we'll explore authentication and authorization by implementing page-level and record-level access control.

## Configuration Files

The first new feature we'll add to our address book is the ability to be configured from an outside configuration file. This will allow us to easily change configurable aspects of our application without having to touch any of the application code. This is helpful during development, but really shines when a non-programmer (like an end-user or a system administrator) needs to change a minor setting when the application is in production.

This feature will also be the easiest to add. Catalyst is set to read configuration from a file by default, and it creates an example configuration file in the application's main directory. In our case, the file is called `addressbook.yml`. This file is in the YAML format, which is convenient for configuration because every data structure in Perl can be described by YAML natively. If you don't like YAML, you can use any configuration file format that `Config::Any` supports. At the time of this writing, that means XML, `Config::General` (Apache-style), INI, JSON, and or a Perl script. To use one of these instead of YAML, just rename the `config` file have an extension that your desired format usually uses (`xml` for XML, `ini` for INI, `js` for JSON, `pl` for Perl, conf for `Config::General`).

The simplest piece of configuration data you can add to your application is a single key/value pair. In YAML syntax, a configuration option `foo` set to `bar` will look like:

```
foo: bar
```

Inside your application, you can access the value of `foo` via the `config` method in the application object:

```
print "Foo is: ". $c->config->{foo};
```

You can also configure individual Components (Models, Views and Controllers) from the `config` file by creating a key with the component type and component name separated by a double colon. For example, the configuration for `MyApp::Model::MyDatabase` would be under the `Model::MyDatabase` key. Setting the key `foo` to value `bar` inside `MyDatabase` would look like the following:

```
Model::MyDatabase:
  foo: bar
```

You can also configure directly inside the class where you use Catalyst :

```
package MyApp;
use Catalyst qw(...);
# ...
__PACKAGE__->config->{Model::MyDatabase} = { foo => 'bar' };
# ...
__PACKAGE__->setup;
1;
```

To get at the from inside `Model::MyDatabase`, you can simply access a piece of class data with the name of the key:

```
$my_foo = $self->{foo};
```

It's better to explicitly create an `accessor` method, though:

```
package MyApp::Model::MyDatabase;
use base 'Catalyst::Model';
__PACKAGE__->mk_ro_accessors('foo');
sub show_foo {
   my $self = shift;
   print "foo is equal to ". $self->foo;
}
```

In this example, we didn't need to access anything from a hash because Catalyst automatically created a (read-only) `accessor` method. The advantage of creating a method to access the data is that mistyping the name in your code somewhere will result in an error (instead of silently returning an undefined value). We also gain the ability to prevent writing, or perhaps return a default value if one isn't specified in the `config` file.

A module called `Class::Accessor::Fast` is used to create the `accessors` (and is where the `mk_ro_accessors` method comes from), so you are free to do anything that is mentioned in the `Class::Accessor` documentation. Catalyst doesn't require you to use `Class::Accessor`, though; you could also write the `accessor/mutator` methods manually, or omit them entirely and just get everything out of the `$self` hash. You are free to do what works best for your application.

# Configuring the Address Book

At this point, our Address Book doesn't have many options to configure. However, there is one critical option: the location of the database. Looking inside `AddressBook::Model::AddressDB`, we can see that the database's location is hard-coded to the value that we initially specified. Fortunately, if we specify a database in the `config` file, it will override the hard-coded value. This means we don't have to modify any code to use a different database; we simply need to add the following option to our `addressbook.yml` file:

```
Model::AddressDB:
  connect_info:
    - DBI:SQLite:__HOME__/database
```

The - in YAML means an "array element" and in DBIC models (like `AddressDB`), the configuration information is an array of four elements. The first element is the DBI connection string. The second and third elements are the database username and password, respectively. The final element is a hash of configuration attributes to pass on to the database driver. `DBIx::Class` and Catalyst don't actually interpret this data, they just pass the array on to a `DBI->connect` call.

As SQLite doesn't use usernames or passwords, we haven't specified them in our configuration.

A configuration entry for a MySQL database (which does use usernames and passwords) would look similar:

```
Model::AddressDB:
  connect_info:
    - DBI:mysql:address_database
    - username
    - password
```

Keep in mind that YAML uses the line's indentation level to determine which keys and values belong to each other. Therefore, it's critical that elements are properly lined up and that only spaces are used to indent rather than tabs.

# Sessions

A feature that almost every web application needs is the ability to store application state for a certain user between requests. HTTP alone treats each request as being completely unrelated to every other request. This is usually undesirable in the context of a web application because some data needs to persist between page loads. For example, it would be very inconvenient to require a user to type his/her username and password on every page to authorize the next action. Sessions are the solution to this problem. When a user first visits your application, Catalyst will supply him/her with a token to identify him/herself for a certain amount of time. Whenever that token is supplied with a request, Catalyst will find its session data and make it accessible in your controllers throughout the request.

To get started with sessions, you'll need to install some modules and load the appropriate session plug-ins into your application. The modules we'll need to install are `Catalyst::Plugin::Session`, `Catalyst::Plugin::Session::State::Cookie`, and `Catalyst::Plugin::Session::Store::FastMmap` or `Catalyst::Plugin::Session::Store::File`.

Catalyst's session engine consists of three parts. The first is `Catalyst::Plugin::Session`, which provides general session functionality. For the session plug-in to work, it needs to be able to do two things—store session data somewhere and be able to get a session id token from each user. The most common form of a token is a cookie that's stored on the user's machine. When your application sets a cookie, the browser will store it and attach it to every request. Catalyst will see this cookie and then restore the appropriate session data. To use cookies to manage sessions, load `Catalyst::Plugin::Session::State::Cookie` into your application.

However, if the user's have disabled cookies for some reason, then this won't work. Nearly every browser and robot on the web today supports cookies, though, so you shouldn't have to worry about browser support. If you absolutely cannot use cookies, try `Catalyst::Plugin::Session::State::URI`, but be aware that it can be buggy because it works by rewriting every link on your generated pages to include the session identifier in the URL. (It can also open up security issues. If a user follows a link to an external website, the external website will be able to retrieve the session id from the `Referrer` header and then steal the user's session. Therefore, it's recommended that you just use cookies.)

Once you have a way to identify each user, you'll need to store the data somewhere. The most convenient method for this is `Catalyst::Plugin::Session::Store::FastMmap`. `FastMmap` will store session data in a memory mapped file, which is fast and efficient but won't be shared between load-balanced machines or persist between runs of your server. (Note that FastMmap won't work on Windows, but you can use `Catalyst::Plugin::Session::Store::File` instead.) Storing the session data in your database will eliminate these problems, but it will be slightly slower. Most real applications won't notice the speed difference. For development, `Session::Store::File` and `Session::Store::FastMmap` are the most convenient as they require no additional configuration.

After you've decided on which `Session::Store` and `Session::State` back-ends to use, simply list them with the other plug-ins. Your `AddressBook.pm` should look something like this:

```
use Catalyst qw/ConfigLoader Static::Simple
          Session Session::State::Cookie Session::Store::FastMmap/;
```

When you restart your application, the first request will result in a cookie being set. Each subsequent request with that cookie will be in the same session. You'll also have access to a few new methods in your context object. The most useful are `$c->session` and `$c->flash`. These methods both work like `$c->stash`, except they persist for more than one request. Data stored with `$c->session` will persist until the session expires (which you can check via the `$c->session_expires` accessor). `$c->flash` is a little bit more complicated. It works like the stash, but will persist between HTTP *redirects* (explained in detail later in this chapter). Once it's read or written to after a redirect, it will be cleared out.

The most convenient way of using the flash is to set:

```
__PACKAGE__->config(session => {flash_to_stash => 1});
```

in `AddressBook.pm` with the rest of your configuration options. With this turned on, the flash from the last request will automatically become the stash for the current request. We'll see how this is helpful in the next section.

# Adding Sessions to the Address Book

Our address book doesn't need sessions in the traditional sense quite yet. It doesn't need to store any data between requests, because nothing is specific to a single user. Every user has the same privileges and every operation changes the data for every other user. However, we can use sessions to improve the user interface.

In the version of AddressBook from Chapter 3, we programmed our `mutator` operations (`/person/delete`, for example) to set a `message` key in the stash and then forward back to the list action. This made deletes seamless—the user just clicked delete and then saw the updated list of people with a message at the top saying that the person had been successfully removed. The only problem was that the URL in the browser was still at `/person/delete/number` instead of `/person/list`. If a user bookmarked that URL assuming that it would lead them to the list of people, they could accidentally delete a person or just get an error message.

Catalyst will let us do better than that. To get the user's URL bar to show the real URL, we need to redirect him (via an HTTP redirection code) to the user list page. If we did that without sessions, everything in the stash would be lost and we wouldn't be able to display a status message at the top of the page. Thanks to the flash though, we can tell Catalyst to display the message on the next page load instead of the current page. All we need to do is enable `flash_to_stash` as above, store the message in `$c->flash`, and issue an HTTP redirect to the user list. Here's the code that implements this for the person deletion action:

```
if($person){
    $c->flash->{message} = 'Deleted ' . $person->name;
    $person->delete;
}
else {
    $c->flash->{error} = "No person $id";
}

$c->response->redirect($c->uri_for('list'));
$c->detach();
```

The only difference between this and the old code is that we are using the flash instead of the stash, and so we redirect instead of forward at the end.

The syntax for redirection might be a bit confusing. Redirection works by setting a header in the HTTP response, and then sending the browser a normal page. As the browser is outside the realm of Catalyst, we have to convert the name of the action to a real fully-qualified URL. We then set the necessary response header ("Location:") to that URL. The `$c->detach()` line will stop all further processing of actions and jump directly to the end action. In this case it's not strictly necessary (since the end action will be called immediately anyway), but if you're inside some if/then statements, detach will get you out as quickly as possible. After you detach, the default end action will see that this response is a redirect and pass that on to the browser without rendering a template.

When the browser requests the `/person/list` page, Catalyst will restore the session, move the flash to the stash, and then handle the request as normal. (If this isn't working for you, make sure you enabled the `flash_to_stash` configuration option as described above.) At the end of the request, the message from the flash will be displayed on top of the page, just like before. This will all be transparent, so you won't have to change the templates at all.

Forwarding will continue to work as before, but you can gradually convert from forwarding to redirection as you see it. Now your users have the best of both worlds. They can bookmark any page and go to the right place, while still receiving informative status messages where necessary.

# Sessions in the Database

If you plan on deploying your application across multiple servers (via a load balancer), putting sessions in the database can make your life easier. You won't need to ensure that each user gets the same server for every request—everything will work perfectly even if the user moves between servers. That means that you can also take servers down without anyone losing data.

The setup isn't quite as simple as with `Session::Store::FastMmap` or `Session::Store::File`, but it is straightforward. The first thing to do is to create a `sessions` table in your database as follows:

```
CREATE TABLE sessions (
        id           CHAR(72) PRIMARY KEY,
        session_data TEXT,
        expires      INTEGER
    );
```

Then, add a schema file, `lib/AddressBook/Schema/AddressDB/Session.pm` to your DBIC schema as follows:

```
package AddressBook::Schema::AddressDB::Session;
use base qw/DBIx::Class/;
__PACKAGE__->load_components(qw/Core/);
__PACKAGE__->table('sessions');
__PACKAGE__->add_columns(
  id =>           { data_type => "CHAR", is_nullable => 0,
                    size => 72 },
  session_data => { data_type => "TEXT", is_nullable => 1,
                    size => undef },
  expires      => { data_type => "INTEGER", is_nullable => 1,
                    size => undef}
);
__PACKAGE__->set_primary_key('id');
1;
```

Then all you have to do is use `Session::Store::DBIC` instead of `Session::Store::FastMmap` and add the following configuration option in `AddressBook.pm`:

```
__PACKAGE__->config( session => {
                                            dbic_class => 'AddressDB::Session',
                                             flash_to_stash => 1 });
```

When you restart your application, session information will be stored in your DBIC model.

# Using Components from Outside Catalyst

As you start using the address book, you might want to be able to import and export data in a standard format. You could add a web interface for this functionality, but sometimes it's easier to just write a quick shell script to parse some outside data and enter it into our database. Thanks to the flexibility of Catalyst, scripts running outside of the main application can use the same Model (and even other components, if you can dream up a use for them) as the application and manipulate the database directly.

Using the `DBIx::Class` schema externally is pretty straightforward. All we need to do is use the Schema, connect to it and add the data.

Let's write a script in the script directory that will accept lines of CSV-formatted data (for example, `"Firstname,Lastname,Home,123 Fake Street,123-456-7890,address@example.com"`) and add them to the database. We start our script by creating it in `script/import_csv.pl` and writing a bit of documentation:

```
#!/usr/bin/perl

=head1 NAME
import_csv.pl - imports CSV files into the address book

=head1 FORMAT

The data should be in CSV format with the following fields:

     firstname, lastname, address location, address, phone, email

=cut
```

Next, we'll load the `Text::CSV_XS` module to parse the CSV data for us.

```
use Text::CSV_XS;
```

Here's the tricky part:

```
use FindBin qw($Bin);
use Path::Class;
use lib dir($Bin, '..', 'lib')->stringify;
```

We want our application to work on any platform and be able to find the configuration file so that we can find the database automatically. We start by using the `FindBin` module to find the filename of our script (placed in the `$Bin` variable). As we put the script in `script/import_csv.pl` and our Catalyst application is rooted one level above, we use the `Path::Class` module to generate the filename of the `lib` directory that's one level above the location of our script. We use `Path::Class` instead of just writing `$Bin/../lib`, so that the script will run under operating systems other than UNIX. Once we have a filename, we pass it to the `lib` pragma to tell Perl to look for modules (our Schema) in that path.

Now we can safely load the schema and YAML to parse the `config` file:

```
use AddressBook::Schema::AddressDB;
use YAML 'LoadFile';
use strict;
```

Here we use the same `FindBin` trick to find the location of our configuration file. We then load it and replace `__HOME__` in the database's path with the root directory of our application (as Catalyst does when it loads the configuration file):

```
my $config = LoadFile(file($Bin, '..', 'addressbook.yml'));
my $dsn    = $config->{'Model::AddressDB'}->{connect_info}->[0];
my $HOME   = dir($Bin, '..');
$dsn =~ s/__HOME__/$HOME/;
```

Our database's connection information in now in `$dsn`, and we can simply connect to the schema:

```
my $schema =
  AddressBook::Schema::AddressDB->connect($dsn)
  or die "Failed to connect to database at $dsn";
```

From there, everything works as it did inside our application, with a few caveats. Instead of using `$c->model('AddressDB::TableName')`, we write `$schema->resultset("TableName")`.

```
while(my $line = <>){
    eval {
   my $csv = Text::CSV_XS->new();
   $csv->parse($line) or die "Invalid data";
   my ($first, $last, $location, $address, $phone, $email)
```

```
            = $csv->fields();
        my $person = $schema->resultset('People')->
          find_or_create({ firstname => $first,
                           lastname  => $last,
                        });
        $schema->resultset('Addresses')->
          create({ person   => $person,
                   location => $location,
                   postal   => $address,
                   phone    => $phone,
                   email    => $email,
                 });
        print "Added @{[$person->name]}'s $location address.\n";
        };
        if($@){
        warn "Problem adding address: $@";
        }
    }
```

The main loop is pretty simple. We first use `Text::CSV_XS` to parse the current line (STDIN or files specified on the command line) into the fields—first name, last name, location, postal address, phone number and email address. We then use the first name and last name to locate an entry in the people table (or create it if it doesn't exist). Then we use that person object to create an appropriate row in the address table, using the rest of the data. If that works, we print out a message saying we added the user and then move on to the next line in the data file.

We also wrap the entire procedure in an `eval{}` block so that we can print an error message and move onto the next piece of data if there's an error.

There's one more thing we need to do before we can run this. The `find_or_create` method will only work if you guarantee to `DBIx::Class` that each firstname and lastname combination is unique. We do this by creating a UNIQUE constraint in the database and then adding the following line to `AddressBook::Schema::AddressDB::People`:

```
    __PACKAGE__->add_unique_constraint(name =>
                                        [qw/firstname lastname/]);
```

This tells `DBIx::Class` that the columns firstname and lastname, taken together, are unique (like a primary key). We name this constraint "name" so that we can distinguish between it and other constraints.

After you add that line to your schema, you should be able to run the application:

```
$ perl script/import_csv.pl
Test,Person,Home,123 Home St.,123-456-7890,home@example.com
Test,Person,Work,123 Work ST.,890-123-4567,work@example.com
^D
$
```

Now when we visit the website, we'll see a Test Person with a Work and Home address! As you can see, sometimes it's very convenient to access your application without a web interface. Some infrequent operations, like reporting or bulk imports, are easier to perform from the command line.

We'll conclude with a script to generate some random CSV data:

```
#!/usr/bin/perl
=head1 NAME
random_addresses.pl - generate random addresses
=head1 USAGE
Run like C<perl script/random_addresses.pl | perl script/import_csv.
pl>
=cut
my @names = qw(Foo Bar Baz Test Jonathan Rockway Person Another A);
my @locations = qw(Home Work Mobile Fax Test);
my @streets = qw(Green Oak Elm 60th Fake State Halsted);
for(1..200){
    my $first = $names[rand @names];
    my $last  = $names[rand @names];
    my $where = $locations[rand @locations];
    my $number = int rand 9900 + 100; # 3-digit street number
    my $street = $streets[rand @streets];
    my $address = "$number $street St.";
    my $phone = join '-', (int rand 800 + 100, int rand 899 + 100,
                      int rand 8999 + 1000);
    my $email = "$first.$last\@$where.example.com";
    print "$first,$last,$where,$address,$phone,$email\n";
}
```

Then we can run:

```
$ perl script/random_addresses.pl | perl script/import_csv.pl
```

When the above command finishes, you'll have 200 new addresses in your database—just in time for the next section on searching!

Thanks to the import script, our application now has all the power of the UNIX command line. Anything that can generate CSV data can now communicate with the application. (You can also try opening up the generated random addresses in your spreadsheet program; it should work fine.)

# Searching and Paging

Now that our application is starting to accumulate a significant quantity of data, it would be nice to be able to search it. In this section, we'll create an interface for searching addresses and names and displaying the search results. We'll start with a form for defining what the user wants to search for:

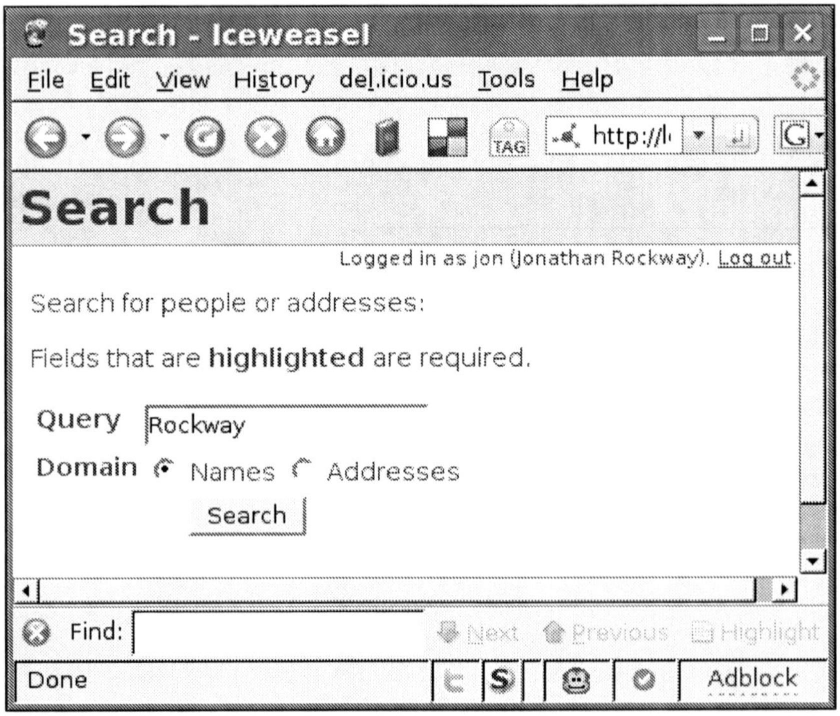

Then we'll search and display the results:

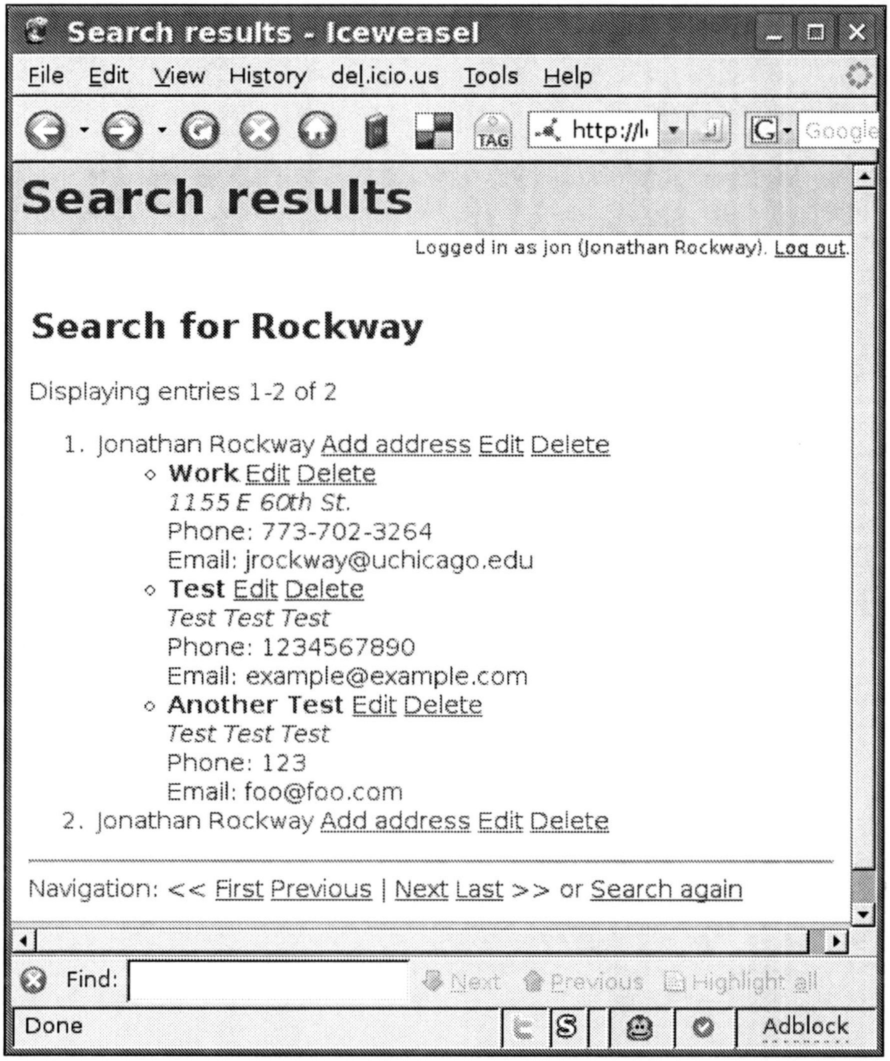


The first thing we'll do is create a Search controller and then write the database logic for searching.

To do this, we'll first create `lib/AddressBook/Controller/Search.pm`. We'll have a single action that will generate a search form and then display results when the form is submitted as follows:

```
package AddressBook::Controller::Search;
use strict;
use warnings;
use base qw(Catalyst::Controller::FormBuilder Catalyst::Controller::
BindLex);
sub search : Global Form {
    my ($self, $c, $query) = @_;
    my $form = $self->formbuilder;

    # get query from the URL (or the form if there's nothing there)
    $query ||= $form->field('query')
      if($form->submitted && $form->validate);

    return unless $query; # no query? we're done

    $c->stash->{query} = $query;
    my @tokens = split /\s+/, $query;
    my $result : Stashed;

    if('Names' eq $form->field('domain')){
              $result = $c->forward('search_names', \@tokens);
              $c->stash->{'template'} = 'search/name_results.tt2'
    }
    else {
              $result = $c->forward('search_addresses', \@tokens);
              $c->stash->{'template'} = 'search/address_results.tt2'
    }

    my $page = $c->request->param('page');
    $page = 1 if($page !~ /^\d+$/);
    $result  = $result->page($page);
    my $pager : Stashed  = $result->pager;
}
```

This is the bulk of the controller. We start by getting a query string from the form or the URL. If the form is empty, we halt further processing and redisplay the form.

If there is a search, we tokenize the search string by splitting the string into an array of words. Our search is going to be a very simple search—it will look for any word in any field. The search will also be limited to either names or addresses, not both. In the next few lines, we determine whether the search domain is addresses or names and forward to a sub-action to actually do the search. When that action returns, we set the necessary template (`name_results` for the name search results, `address_results` otherwise).

Finally, we'll account for paging the results. Instead of displaying every result on one page, we'll split it up to show only 10 results per page. To do this, we simply call the `page` method on the resultset. Page will return a new resultset that will only contain 10 results. Also, if there's a numeric "page" parameter set in the URL, we'll skip to that page of the resultset (`$page`). Otherwise, we'll display the first page.

Lastly, we'll get a "pager" for this resultset. The pager is a `Data::Page` object and stores metadata about the paged resultset. It will allow us to easily create links to the first page of results, last page, next page, and previous page, and also contains the number of results on this page, the total number of results, the total number of pages, etc. You could manually calculate these things, but it's tricky and time consuming to get it right. Catalyst and `DBIx::Class` will handle all the tedious details of paging results automatically.

That's the bulk of our search. The next methods send the actual search requests to the database:

```
sub search_addresses : Private {
    my ($self, $c, @tokens) = @_;
    my @address_fields = qw/postal phone email location/;
    @address_fields    = cross(\@address_fields, \@tokens);
    return $c->model('AddressDB::Addresses')->
search(\@address_fields);
}
sub search_names : Private {
    my ($self, $c, @tokens) = @_;
    my @people_fields = qw/firstname lastname/;
    @people_fields    = cross(\@people_fields, \@tokens);
    return $c->model('AddressDB::People')->

search(\@people_fields);
}
sub cross {
    my $columns = shift || [];
    my $tokens  = shift || [];
    map {s/%/\\%/g} @$tokens;

    my @result;
    foreach my $column (@$columns){
         push @result,
              (map +{$column => {-like => "%$_%"}}, @$tokens);
    }
    return @result;
}
1; # End the module with a true value!
```

Most of the work is done in the `cross` subroutine, which generates a list of all columns paired with all the search tokens. As we're doing a text search, we want to use the `LIKE` predicate and enclose the terms in `%`. The SQL we want for a name search of "Test Person" is:

```
SELECT * FROM people WHERE firstname LIKE '%Test%' OR
firstname LIKE '%Person%' OR lastname LIKE '%Person%' OR
lastname LIKE '%Test';
```

In `DBIx::Class` notation, we want:

```
$c->model('AddressDB::People')->
   search([{ firstname => {-like => '%Test%'}},
           { firstname => {-like => '%Person%'}},
           { lastname  => {-like => '%Test%'}},
           { lastname  => {-like => '%Person%'}}]);
```

The cross routine simply returns the part that's inside of `search([])`.

Now that our logic is configured, we just need to generate the HTML. As with the forms in the last chapter, we'll use FormBuilder to automatically generate the search page. First, we'll create a `root/forms/search/search.fb` form as follows:

```
name: search
method: GET
header: 1
title: Search
fields:
  query:
    label: Query
    type: text
    required: 1
  domain:
    label: Domain
    options: Names, Addresses
    required: 1
submit: Search
```

We're using the `GET` method this time so that we can redo the search (via the results page) for each page. The first page will be at the URL `/search?query=Something`, the second page will be at `/search?query=Something&page=2`, etc. We need the basic template to display this form as well:

```
[% META title="Search" %]
Search for people or addresses:
[% FormBuilder.render %]
```

As you'd expect, that file lives in `root/src/search/search.tt2`.

The next thing to take care of is the results page. As the name results and address results pages are very similar, we're going to create a **wrapper** template that those two results will include. We'll just put it in `root/src/search/results_wrapper.tt2` so we can include it in the real templates with a minimum of effort. Here's the code:

```
<h2>Search for [% query | html %]</h2>
<p>Displaying entries [% pager.first %]-[% pager.last %] of
[% pager.total_entries %]</p>
<ol start="[% pager.first %]">
[% content %]
</ol>
<hr />
Navigation:
&lt;&lt;
<a href="[% Catalyst.req.uri_with({ page => pager.first_page })
%]">First</a>
<a href="[% Catalyst.req.uri_with({ page => pager.previous_page
})%]">Previous</a>
|
<a href="[% Catalyst.req.uri_with({ page => pager.next_page
})%]">Next</a>
<a href="[% Catalyst.req.uri_with({ page => pager.last_page })
%]">Last</a>
 &gt;&gt;
or <a href="[% Catalyst.uri_for('/search') %]">Search again</a>
```

This template is actually where most of the interesting stuff happens. At the top, we use the pager object to provide some information about which page we're on, how many results there are, etc. Then we start a numbered list at the first result on this page and include the content from the real template. After the real template (the template that actually displays the search results), we generate all the necessary navigation links. The key to this is the `$c->response->uri_with` (`[% Catalyst.res.uri_with( ... ) %]` inside the template) method. This method accepts a list of query string parameters (page in this case) and will replace the parameter with the provided replacement, keeping the rest of the URL the same as the current page. In this case, if we're at `http://localhost:3000/search?domain=Names&query=Some+Names+That+I+Like&page=5`, `[% Catalyst.res,uri_with({ page => 15 }) %]` would result in the URL `http://localhost:3000/search?domain=Names&query=Some+Names+That+I+Like&page=15`. This makes it very simple to modify the current URL—you don't need to parse anything.

We use `uri_with` four times, twice to generate the URLs for the first and last pages of the result, and twice to generate links to the next and previous pages of the results. A more polished application might want to hide the links for pages that don't exist (there's no next page when you're on the last page, for example).

Now we just need to create the two templates to display the results. We're going to copy the display logic from the template that displays the list of all people and their addresses. To make it easier to maintain our templates, we're going to extract the code that displays a single person and the code that displays a single address to separate templates. We'll then include that code from the `list.tt2` template and `name_results.tt2` and `address_results.tt2`.

The first template will display an address stored in a variable called "address":

```
<b>[% address.location | html  %]</b>
<a href="[% Catalyst.uri_for("/address/edit/$address.id") %]">
  Edit</a>
<a href="[% Catalyst.uri_for("/address/delete/$address.id") %]">
Delete</a>
<br />
<address>[% address.postal | html | html_line_break %]</address>
    Phone: [% address.phone | html %]<br />
    Email: [% address.email | html %]<br />
```

We'll store this in `root/src/address_fragment.tt2`, so it's clear that this is just a fragment of a page. Next is the `person_fragment.tt2` template, which will display a person (and his addresses) stored in a variable named "person":

```
[% person.name | html %]
<a href="[% Catalyst.uri_for("/address/add/$person.id")
   | html %]">Add address</a>
<a href="[% Catalyst.uri_for("/person/edit/$person.id")
   | html %]">Edit</a>
<a href="[% Catalyst.uri_for("/person/delete/$person.id")
   | html %]">Delete</a>
[% SET addresses = person.addresses %]
<ul>
[% FOREACH address = addresses %]
 <li>[% INCLUDE address_fragment.tt2 %]</li>
[% END %]
</ul>
```

Note that we're including the `address_fragment.tt2` template for every address that a person has. It's important to note that the address variable from this template will exist inside the template we include and that it's possible for the included templates to modify variables in the calling template. If you'd rather not want this to happen, use the `[% PROCESS %]` directive instead.

Let us modify `root/src/person/list.tt2` to use the new fragments by replacing the existing `WHILE` loop with the following:

```
[% WHILE (person = people.next) %]
  <li>[% INCLUDE person_fragment.tt2 %]</li>
[% END %]
```

This cleans up the code quite nicely. We're finally ready to create the search results templates:

First, `root/src/search/name_results.tt2`

```
[% META title = "Search results" %]
[% WRAPPER "search/results_wrapper.tt2" %]
[% WHILE (person = result.next) %]
<li>[% INCLUDE person_fragment.tt2 %]</li>
[% END %]
[% END %]
```

Next, `root/src/search/address_results.tt2`

```
[% META title = "Search results" %]
[% WRAPPER "search/results_wrapper.tt2" %]
[% WHILE (address = result.next) %]
<li>[% address.location | html %] address for [% address.person.name
%]<br />
[% INCLUDE address_fragment.tt2 %]
</li>
[% END %]
[% END %]
```

Factoring templates into small fragments make it very easy to modify something once and have it appear everywhere in your application. There's no code to cut-n-paste if you want the layout of both result pages to change. Just modify the wrapper and both pages will look the same.

Writing these templates was the final step to get the searching working. You should be able to start your application, navigate to `/search`, and search to your heart's content. If you need more data in your database, just run the `import_csv.pl` script again.

# Authentication and Authorization

Now that our application has some real data in it, it would be nice to only show it to the authorized users, not everyone on the Internet. In Catalyst, this is a two step process. First, we use **Authentication** plug-ins to determine who a user is. In the simplest case, we ask the user to enter a username and password. If the username is known and the password is correct, we assume that the person at the other end of the connection is the user whose username they specified. If we wanted to be more flexible, we could ask users to log in with OpenID, their Flickr username and password, or Bitcard. Either way, the end result is that we can authoritatively associate a username with the session and then act on that username to grant permission to restricted areas of our application. The granting of permission is the second stage—**Authorization**.

## Authentication

As with sessions, Catalyst handles Authentication via an array of plug-ins. The main plug-in is `Catalyst::Plugin::Authentication`. This plug-in calls upon sub-plugins that handle the various details, such as reading the OpenID credentials or looking up a username and password in the database. Regardless of the plug-ins you use, you'll get a standard interface. Every logged in user gets a user object, accessible through `$c->user->obj`. If you use DBIC to store your usernames and passwords, this object is a full DBIC resultset for the user's row in the user table. This will allow you to store user preferences in the database right next to their username and password, as well as create relations to other tables. Other back-ends might not put anything in the object, but the username will always be available via `$c->user`.

The simplest way to try authentication in your application is via the "Minimal" back-end, with a setup like the following in your application's main file:

```
use Catalyst qw/
            Authentication
            Authentication::Store::Minimal
            Authentication::Credential::Password
            # (use the same session settings as before)
            Session Sesion::Store::... Session::State::...
            /;
__PACKAGE__->config->{authentication}{users} = {
   username => {
      password => "password",
      roles    => [qw/may_view may_edit/],
   }
};
```

This will store usernames and passwords directly in the configuration file. This makes testing very easy, since you can add any attributes to the user object by specifying keys and values alongside the password or roles without having to change your database schema. Another easy way to get authentication going quickly is to generate an Apache `htpasswd` file and use `Authentication::Store::Htpasswd`:

```
use Catalyst qw/
                Authentication
                Authentication::Store::Htpasswd
                Authentication::Credential::Password
                Session Session::Store::... Session::State::...
                /;
__PACKAGE__->config->{authentication}{htpasswd}
                                = "/path/to/passwd.file";
```

Once you have an authentication store and some users, you can create an action that reads the username and password from the user and calls `$c->login($username, $password)`. If the username and password were correct, `$c->login` will return true and store that fact in the session so the user doesn't have to re-authenticate to every page. Once the user is logged in, your actions can test `$c->user` and act upon the information as they see it. When the user is done with his session, your application should call `$c->logout`, which will delete the session data.

## Authorization

Having just a username isn't particularly useful, unless your application only wants to differentiate between logged in users and anonymous users. If you'd like to apply different rules to different classes of users for different URLs, you'll want to use some of the Catalyst's Authorization plug-ins.

The simplest Authorization plug-in is `Authorization::Roles`. This plug-in provides methods for testing if a user belongs to a certain "role", or class, of users. You'll need a back end that supports roles, but fortunately both the Minimal back end and the DBIC back end do. Using roles is very simple. At the beginning of your action, you call `$c->assert_user_roles(qw/role1 role2/)`. This method will throw an exception unless the user is a member of both role1 and role2. For example, an action called `edit_management_reports` might look like this:

```
sub edit_management_reports {
  my ($self, $c) = @_;
  $c->assert_user_roles(qw/manager editor/);
  generate_reports();
}
```

Unless a user is both a manager and an editor, the `generate_reports()` command will never be called. The user will instead get an *access denied* error message.

`$c->assert_user_role(qw/role1 role2/)` works similarly, but only requires a user to possess one of the mentioned roles (not all). If you want more control over what happens when a user is denied access, you can use `$c->check_user_role(s)` instead. These methods work like `assert_user_role(s)`, but returns true if the check succeeds and returns false otherwise. You can check the result in an `if` statement, and act accordingly:

```
if($c->check_user_role(qw|administrator editor|)){
  do_the_edit();
}
else {
  $c->stash->{error} = "You are not authorized to edit this.";
  $c->detach('/denied');
}
```

This is the most basic way to use roles to control access. A more flexible option is the `Authorization::ACL` plug-in. This plug-in allows you to setup per-path rules that are tested on each request. If all of the checks pass, the user is allowed to access the page. Otherwise, an `/access_denied` method is executed instead. This method can display an error to the user, or check some other credentials and allow access anyway.

For example, to use the ACL to disallow access to `/admin` for non-administrators, your `MyApp.pm (or AddressBook.pm)` file will look like the following:

```
use Catalyst qw/ConfigLoader Static::Simple
          Session Session::State::Cookie Session::Store::DBIC
                Authentication
                Authentication::Store::DBIC
                Authentication::Credential::Password
                     Authorization::Roles
                     Authorization::ACL/;
# setup sessions, authorization, and authentication
## ACL rules
__PACKAGE__->deny_access_unless('/admin', [qw/admin/]);
```

This code will check the user's role on every request to `/admin`. If the user isn't in all of the listed roles (only 'admin' in this case), then the request goes to `/access_denied` instead of `/admin`. This rule will also apply to `/admin/list/user/123` and anything in a path below `/admin`.

If you prefer not to use roles, you can also use an arbitrary subroutine:

```
__PACKAGE__->allow_access_if(
    '/bonus/area',
            sub { my ($c, $action) = @_;
             if($c->user->karma > 50){
                 return $ALLOWED
             }
             else {
                 return $DENIED
             }
         }
    );
```

Here we allow access to `/bonus/area` only if the user has a karma (as defined by the user object) greater than 50. Otherwise, the `/access_denied` action is run instead.

The ACL plug-in gives you the ability to easily apply arbitrary rules to an entire portion of your application, without having to change any controller code.

# Adding Authentication and Authorization to the Address Book

Now that we've had an overview of authentication and authorization, let's restrict access to our address book. To make the management of users and roles as easy as possible, we'll store the user data and role data in our DBIC model. For now, we'll manually add users to the database and set their usernames and passwords. We'll also optionally associate an entry in the person table with each user, to allow non-editors to edit their own addresses. Finally, we'll create two roles, "viewer" and "editor" and restrict access to the site via an ACL. We'll let viewers view any data and allow editors to mutate that data (edit/create/delete). Also, we'll make an exception—if a user is a viewer but wants to add or delete his own addresses, we'll allow that.

The first step is to create the necessary tables in our database:

```
$ sqlite3 database
CREATE TABLE user (id INTEGER PRIMARY KEY, username TEXT, password TEXT,
person INTEGER);
INSERT INTO user VALUES(1, 'edit', 'editme', 1);
INSERT INTO user VALUES(2, 'view', 'viewme', 2);
CREATE TABLE role (
        id   INTEGER PRIMARY KEY,
```

```
        role TEXT
    );
INSERT INTO role VALUES(1, 'editor');
INSERT INTO role VALUES(2, 'viewer');
CREATE TABLE user_role (
        user INTEGER REFERENCES user,
        role INTEGER REFERENCES role,
        PRIMARY KEY (user, role)
    );
INSERT INTO user_role VALUES(1, 1);
INSERT INTO user_role VALUES(1, 2);
INSERT INTO user_role VALUES(2, 2);
DELETE FROM people; -- Clear out the database
INSERT INTO people VALUES(1, 'Editor', 'Person');
INSERT INTO people VALUES(2, 'Viewer', 'Person');
```

Here, we created three tables, a user table to store username, passwords and the link to the people table; a role table to store a list of roles; and a `user_role` table to apply roles to each user. Then we added two users, "edit" and "view" (with passwords "editme" and "viewme" respectively. (Note that we're using cleartext passwords for testing. When we deploy the application, we'll encrypt the password so that the passwords are not revealed if the database is stolen.) We also added "editor" and "viewer" roles and made "edit" a member of the "editor" and "viewer" role, and "view" only a "viewer". Finally, we created the entries in the people table for each user.

Next we'll need to create three schema files in `lib/AddressBook/Schema/AddressDB` as follows:

```
package AddressBook::Schema::AddressDB::User;
use strict;
use base 'DBIx::Class';
__PACKAGE__->load_components( qw/ Core / );
__PACKAGE__->table('user');
__PACKAGE__->add_columns( id =>        { data_type => "INTEGER" },
                  username => { data_type => "TEXT" },
                  password => { data_type => "TEXT" },
                  person   => { data_type => "INTEGER"}, );
__PACKAGE__->set_primary_key( 'id' );
__PACKAGE__->has_many(map_user_role =>
               'AddressBook::Schema::AddressDB::UserRole' => 'user');
```

```
__PACKAGE__->belongs_to(person => 'AddressBook::Schema::AddressDB::
People');

1;

package AddressBook::Schema::AddressDB::Role;
use strict;
use base 'DBIx::Class';

__PACKAGE__->load_components( qw/ Core / );
__PACKAGE__->table( 'role' );
__PACKAGE__->add_columns( id   => { data_type => "INTEGER" },
                          role => { data_type => "TEXT" },
                        );
__PACKAGE__->set_primary_key( 'id' );
__PACKAGE__->has_many( map_user_role =>
                        'AddressBook::Schema::AddressDB::UserRole' => 'role'
);

1;

package AddressBook::Schema::AddressDB::UserRole;
use strict;
use base 'DBIx::Class';

__PACKAGE__->load_components( qw/ Core / );
__PACKAGE__->table( 'user_role' );
__PACKAGE__->add_columns( user => {data_type => "INTEGER"},
                          role => {data_type => "INTEGER"},);
__PACKAGE__->set_primary_key( qw/user role/ );

1;
```

Now we just need to configure the application to use these schemata in `AddressBook.pm` as follows:

```
use Catalyst qw/ConfigLoader Static::Simple
          Session Session::State::Cookie Session::Store::DBIC
                 Authentication
                 Authentication::Store::DBIC
                 Authentication::Credential::Password
          Authorization::Roles
          Authorization::ACL/;

__PACKAGE__->config( name => 'AddressBook' );

__PACKAGE__->config( session => {
                        dbic_class => 'AddressDB::Session',
                        expires    => 3600,
                        flash_to_stash => 1,
                       }
               );
```

```
__PACKAGE__->config->{authentication}{dbic} =
  {
   user_class    => 'AddressDB::User',
   user_field    => 'username',
   password_type => 'clear', # use salted_hash for real applications
  };
__PACKAGE__->config->{authorization}{dbic} =
  {
   role_class           => 'AddressDB::Role',
   role_field           => 'role',
   role_rel             => 'map_user_role',
   user_role_user_field => 'user',
  };
# Start the application
__PACKAGE__->setup;
```

Now our application is set to use authentication information from the database and we're ready to start implementing the guts of our authentication infrastructure. We'll first need to change the use base line in `AddressBook::Controller::Root` as follows:

```
use base qw(Catalyst::Controller::FormBuilder Catalyst::Controller::
BindLex);
```

Then we need to create `login`, `logout` and `access_denied` methods as follows:

```
sub access_denied : Private {
    my ($self, $c) = @_;
    $c->stash->{template} = 'denied.tt2';
}
sub login : Global Form {
  my ($self, $c) = @_;
  my $form = $self->formbuilder;
  return unless $form->submitted && $form->validate;
   if($c->login($form->field('username'),
                 $form->field('password')))
  {
         $c->flash->{message} = 'Logged in successfully.';
         $c->res->redirect($c->uri_for('/'));
         $c->detach();
   }
   else {
        $c->stash->{error} = 'Login failed.';
   }
```

```
}
sub logout : Global {
    my ($self, $c) = @_;
    $c->logout;
    $c->flash->{message} = 'Logged out.';
    $c->res->redirect($c->uri_for('/'));
}
```

These three actions are very simple. `access_denied` just displays the access denied template when the user isn't authorized to access a certain page. logout calls `$c->logout` and redirects the user to the main page, with a message saying that the logout has succeeded. Finally, login reads in a FormBuilder form and checks the provided username and password. If it matches a user database, the login succeeds. If it doesn't match then we let the user try again, while displaying an error message on top of the login form.

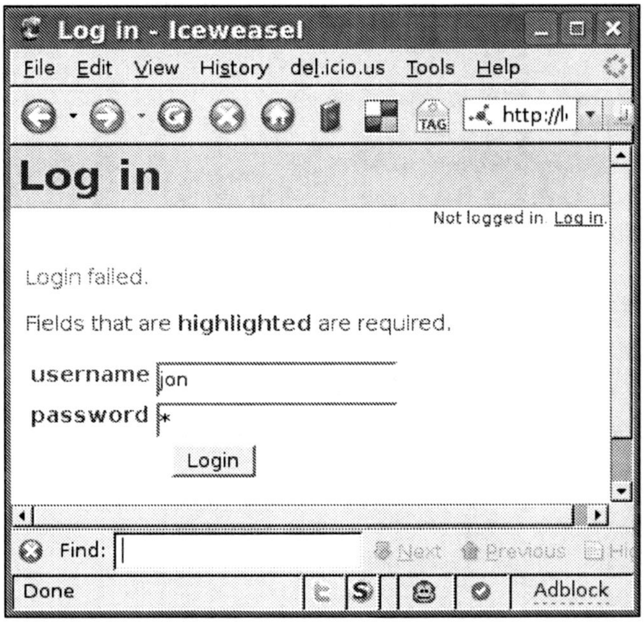


The login form and login template go in the usual places, `root/forms/login.fb` for the form definition and `root/src/login.tt2` for the template and are very similar to the forms and templates we've already created:

```
[% META title="Log in" %]
[% FormBuilder.render %]
```

```
name: login
method: POST
```

```
header: 1
title: Login
fields:
  username:
    label: username
    type: text
    required: 1
  password:
    label: password
    type: password
    required: 1
submit: Login
```

We'll also modify our global header in `root/lib/site/layout` to show the logged in user's name:

```
<div id="header">[% PROCESS site/header %]</div>
<div id="userinfo">
  [% IF Catalyst.user %]
    Logged in as [% Catalyst.user -%]
  [%- IF Catalyst.user.person.name -%]
  ([% Catalyst.user.person.name %])
  [%- END %].
  <a href="[% Catalyst.uri_for('/logout') %]">Log out</a>.
  [% ELSE %]
    Not logged in.  <a href="[% Catalyst.uri_for('/login') %]">Log
in</a>.
  [% END %]
</div>
<div id="content">
```

Note that the first and last lines should already exist in the file. We'll also need to update the CSS (`root/src/ttsite.css`) a bit, so that the username displays in a small font on the right side of the screen:

```
#userinfo {
    font-size: .8em;
    text-align: right;
}
```

Upon restarting the server, you should be able to visit `/login`, type in a username and password and be logged in! Clicking the logout link should cause Catalyst to forget that you logged in (and allow you to log in again). With that working, we're ready to add the final feature—*authorization*.

We'll implement authorization in two stages. First, we'll add generic rules to only allow viewers to view pages that contain address data. To the end of `AddressBook.pm`, after `__PACKAGE__->setup`, add the following:

```
## ACLs
__PACKAGE__->deny_access_unless('/person', [qw/viewer/]);
__PACKAGE__->deny_access_unless('/search', [qw/viewer/]);
__PACKAGE__->deny_access_unless('/address', [qw/viewer/]);

# should always be allowed
__PACKAGE__->allow_access('/index');
__PACKAGE__->allow_access('/login');
```

We'll also need the template to display when the user is denied access, `root/src/denied.tt2`:

```
[% META title="Access denied" %]

[% IF !error %]You are not allowed to access this resource.[% END %]
[% IF !Catalyst.user %]
<a href="[% Catalyst.uri_for('/login') %]">Logging in</a> might help.
[% END %]
```

This template does a few different things. If the user's not logged in, then the page suggests that the user should authenticate and then try again. If an error message has been specified, then that's displayed. Otherwise, a default message is displayed: *You are not allowed to access this resource.*

The final step is to add a rule to all edit actions to see if a user is a member of the editor role, or she/he's editing his own entry. So, at the top of each editing action, add some code like the following:

```
# check ACL
$address = $c->model('AddressDB::Address')->...
if($address->person->id != eval{$c->user->person->id} &&
   !$c->check_any_user_role('editor')){
        $c->stash->{error} =
          'You are not authorized to delete addresses
          for this person.';

        $c->detach('/access_denied');
   }
```

We're using the `eval` statement to protect against the case where `$c->user` doesn't exist (and calling person on an undefined value would make the program die).

You'll want to add this to the edit and delete actions in `AddressBook::Controller::Person` and `AddressBook::Controller::Address`, modifying the error message as appropriate. You also might want to disallow a user from deleting his/her name, as that will cause the foreign key in the user table to dangle into nowhere.

When you've made those changes, fire up the application and explore the robust access control system that you've created!

# Summary

In this chapter, we added some of the most common features that web applications need to our address book application. We learned how to make deployment easy by using the configuration file. Next, we saw how to store data between requests with Session plug-ins, and how to use the Session plug-in to make the user's experience more consistent and enjoyable. We also learned how to identify users and use their identity to control access to the application. Later, we programmed search logic and learned how to display resultsets that span multiple pages. Finally, we learned how to utilize our application's model outside of our application.

# 5
# Building a More Advanced Application

In this chapter, we'll build a brand new application from scratch while exploring the advanced features of Catalyst, `DBIx::Class` and the Template Toolkit. We'll start by modelling our data and building a `DBIx::Class` schema. Then we'll add some extra code to the schema to abstract away some more complex queries. After that we'll build a web interface to the database with just a few lines of code. Finally, we'll add some editing features to the web interface.

## The Application

The application we'll be building in this chapter is called ChatStat and arises from a need to track the opinions of `irc.perl.org` denizens. A common convention on `irc.perl.org` is to add `++` or `--` and a quip after a word. These one-liners are usually amusing and deserve to live on after they've scrolled off the screen. So, we'll write a Catalyst application to make this data available on the web.

## Background

Before we set up the data model, it's important to understand what data we need to keep track of. The most important piece of data to track is the actual opinions from the IRC channel. A complete opinion on IRC looks something like the following:

```
(on #channel) < nickname> (some thing)++ # things are good
```

Here we see `nickname` saying that he likes `some thing` on `#channel` because `things are good`. In our database, we'll want to store each opinion as a parsed entity consisting of columns for the `channel`, the `nickname`, the `thing` ("some thing" here), how many points were given (1 for "++", 0 for "+-", and -1 for "--"), the comment ("things are good") and, finally the entire message (so that we can fix up the other columns if we find our parser not working properly later).

For the sake of making queries easier to write, we'll also normalize the data. This means that there will be a `things` table that gives each `thing` a unique ID and similar tables for the nicknames and channels. This will result in an opinions table that has records like "57, 42, 89, 6, 1, 'message' and 'something++ # message'". 57 is the (opinion) primary key, 42 is the nickname primary key, 89 is the thing primary key, 6 is the channel, etc. Database management systems work best with this sort of data (as redundancy is eliminated) and it makes it easy to add metadata to the entities later. (A nickname will consist of a hostname, username and nickname; a channel will consist of an IRC network and channel names, etc.) Normalizing the data means that it's simple to add extra metadata later, without affecting the existing queries.

Finally, since one person (in real life) can have multiple nicknames, we'll add a person table to group related nicknames together. Each nickname will *belong to* one person.

# Creating the Database

First, we'll create the application so that we have some place to put our database file. We won't be doing much with Catalyst to start, but we'll need the project eventually:

```
$ catalyst.pl ChatStat
$ cd ChatStat
```

Let's get started by creating the tables in SQLite as follows:

```
$ sqlite3 root/database
    CREATE TABLE channels (
      cid INTEGER PRIMARY KEY NOT NULL,
      channel TEXT NOT NULL
    );
    CREATE TABLE nicknames (
      nid INTEGER PRIMARY KEY NOT NULL,
      pid INTEGER NOT NULL,
      nick TEXT NOT NULL,
      username TEXT NOT NULL,
      host TEXT NOT NULL
    );
```

```
CREATE TABLE opinions (
  oid INTEGER PRIMARY KEY NOT NULL,
  nid INTEGER NOT NULL,
  cid INTEGER NOT NULL,
  tid INTEGER NOT NULL,
  message TEXT NOT NULL,
  reason TEXT NOT NULL,
  points INTEGER NOT NULL
);
CREATE TABLE people (
  pid INTEGER PRIMARY KEY NOT NULL,
  name TEXT NOT NULL
);
CREATE TABLE things (
  tid INTEGER PRIMARY KEY NOT NULL,
  thing TEXT NOT NULL
);
CREATE UNIQUE INDEX channel_channels on channels (channel);
CREATE UNIQUE INDEX hostmask_nicknames on nicknames (nick, username,
host);
CREATE UNIQUE INDEX nickname_people on people (name);
CREATE UNIQUE INDEX thing_things on things (thing);
CREATE INDEX idx_opinions_tid ON opinions (tid);
```

The tables are pretty straightforward, but note that we are creating some unique indices for various columns. This ensures that we can't accidentally give a `thing` multiple ID numbers and end up with a useless opinions table. It also makes writing the database code easier; we can look up a thing by its name instead of its unique ID (primary key), as the database guarantees that each `thing` will only appear in the things table once. The `hostmask_nicknames` index is a bit different; the data we get from IRC is in the form (nick, username, and host) so that the index will let us retrieve the unique ID given to that data.

Finally, we have a regular index on `opinions.tid`. We'll be grouping by this column in many queries, so it's logical to index. Doing so reduces the runtime of some queries from two seconds per query to thirty or more queries per second!

Now that we have the tables in place, we'll need to generate a `DBIx::Class` schema and add the relationships:

```
$ perl script/app_ircxory_create.pl model DBIC DBIC::Schema
ChatStat::Schema create=static DBI:SQLite:root/database
```

This will create the files in `lib/ChatStat/Schema/*`. Let us look at those files one-at-a-time and add the constraints.

First, let us look at `People.pm`. All we need to add here is a name for our unique constraint and a line telling `DBIx::Class` that a person can have many nicknames.

Here's the constraint:

```
__PACKAGE__->add_unique_constraint(
  nickname => [qw/name/]
);
```

This will allow us to write the following:

```
my $jrockway = $people->find('jrockway',
                             { key => 'nickname' });
```

Later in the app, it's ensured that a UNIQUE INDEX over name will be created when we redeploy the schema.

Here's the `has_many` relationship:

```
__PACKAGE__->has_many(
  "nicknames",
  "ChatStat::Schema::Nicknames",
  { "foreign.pid" => "self.pid" },
);
```

This command will tell `DBIx::Class` to create an accessor called "nicknames" that will return an array of `ChatStat::Schema::Nickname` objects. The third argument is the join condition specified in `SQL::Abstract` syntax. In this case, we say to join on `people.pid = nicknames.pid`.

`Nicknames.pm` will look similar. We have another unique constraint, a `has_many` relationship to opinions (every nickname has many opinions), and a `belongs_to` relationship back to People. The `belongs_to` relationship, will allow us to access the person record when we only have a nickname.

Here's the code:

```
__PACKAGE__->add_unique_constraint(
  hostmask => [qw/nick username host/]
);
__PACKAGE__->has_many(
  "opinions",
  "ChatStat::Schema::Opinions",
  { "foreign.nid" => "self.nid" },
);
__PACKAGE__->belongs_to(
  "person",
```

```
    "ChatStat::Schema::People",
    { pid => "pid" }
);
```

The has_many relationship looks the same as the one we just created.

The belongs_to relationship is also similar. We say to create a person accessor that will return a ChatStat::Schema::People object for the person. We've also abbreviated the join condition here, omitting the reference to foreign and self because foreign and self are implied automatically when they're omitted and there are no other conditions. It saves a bit of typing.

Moving along, let's take a look at the Things.pm file. We're going to add another unique constraint and has_many relationship here:

```
__PACKAGE__->add_unique_constraint(
    thing => [qw/thing/]
);
__PACKAGE__->has_many(
    "opinions",
    "ChatStat::Schema::Opinions",
    { "foreign.tid" => "self.tid" },
);
```

By now this pattern should be looking familiar. The has_many relationship will create an opinions accessor that will return a list of opinions that relate to the current "thing".

Channels.pm is going to look almost exactly the same:

```
__PACKAGE__->add_unique_constraint(
    channel => [qw/channel/]
);
__PACKAGE__->has_many(
    "opinions",
    "ChatStat::Schema::Opinions",
    { "foreign.cid" => "self.cid" },
);
```

Finally, we'll edit Opinions.pm and add belongs_to relationships to reverse the has_many relationships we created above:

```
__PACKAGE__->belongs_to(
    "nickname",
    "ChatStat::Schema::Nicknames",
    { nid => "nid" },
);
```

```
__PACKAGE__->belongs_to(
  "thing",
  "ChatStat::Schema::Things",
  { tid => "tid" },
);
__PACKAGE__->belongs_to(
  "channel",
  "ChatStat::Schema::Channels",
  { cid => "cid" },
);
```

That's all we need to do. Now every piece of data is related properly, allowing us to get whatever data is needed in a Perl fashion. Setting up a normalized schema is a bit more work, but the data is more organized and working with it using `DBIx::Class` will be a pleasure.

# Populating the Database

An empty database isn't much fun, so let's add some data to it. In the version of this application that I use, I have a POE-based IRCBot dynamically added data to the database as messages come in from IRC. As POE is beyond the scope of this book, we'll create a small command-line script that works similarly. For the curious, the IRCBot code is included with the book and lives under the `ChatStat::Robot` namespace.

For the data-adding script, we'll take the same approach as the IRCBot. We'll start with a string that looks like an IRC message, parse it into its components and then add it to the database.

Let us start with a class to abstract the components of the message. In `lib/ChatStat/Action.pm`, create the following:

```
package ChatStat::Action;
use strict;
use warnings;
use Regexp::Common qw/balanced/;
use base 'Class::Accessor';
__PACKAGE__->mk_accessors(qw|who channel word points reason message|);
use Readonly;
Readonly my %OP_POINTS => ( '++' => 1,
                            '--' => -1,
                            '-+' => 0,
                            '+-' => 0,
                          );
```

```
sub new {
    my ($class, $who, $where, $what) = @_;
    my $self = $class->SUPER::new({ who      => $who,
                                    channel  => $where,
                                    message  => $what
                                  });

    $self->_parse;
    return $self;
}

sub _parse {
    my $self = shift;
    my $what = $self->message;

    my $parens =  $RE{balanced}{-parens=>'(){}[]<>'}{-keep};
    if ($what =~ /
         (?:                        # what we're voting on:
                $parens             # something in parens
                |                   #  -or-
                ([A-Za-z_:0-9]+)    # a single word++
         )
         ([+-]{2})                  # the operation (inc or dec)
           \s*                      # spaces, who cares
         (?:[#] \s* (.+)$)?         # and an optional reason
                /x
       )
      {
          my $paren  = $1;
          my $word   = $2;
          if (defined $paren) {
              $paren =~ s/^[({[<]//;
              $paren =~ s/[)}\]>]$//;
              $word = $paren;
          }
          my $op     = $3;
          my $reason = $4;
          $reason = '' if !defined $reason;
          # trim
          $word   =~ s/^\s+//;
          $word   =~ s/\s+$//;
          $reason =~ s/^\s+//;
          $reason =~ s/\s+$//;
          # it worked
          $self->word(lc $word);
```

```
            $self->reason(lc $reason);
            $self->points($OP_POINTS{$op} || 0);
            return;
        }
    die 'parse error';
}
1;
```

This class takes a nickname, channel name and message, and sets up a data structure consisting of the parsed-out parts. For example, when you invoke:

```
my $a = ChatStat::Action->new('jon', '#test',
                              'Catalyst++ # fun');
```

You'll be able to access the components like the following:

```
my $nick   = $a->who;    # jon
my $points = $a->points; # 1 (-1 if we said --)
my $reason = $a->reason; # fun
my $word   = $a->word;   # catalyst
```

We use `Regexp::Common` to parse out balanced sets of parentheses so that we can add points to a phrase like "a phrase" by typing "(a phrase) ++". Thanks to `Regexp::Common::balanced`, we can use any paired brackets we want, like `<something>++` or `{something else}--`.

With the parsing out of the way, we want to be able to add one of these Actions to the database. Because of the normalized schema, we have to do some extra work. We need to create the "dependencies" of the opinion first (thing, nickname, and channel) and then insert the actual opinion record. The nickname object is created similarly as it needs to refer to an existing person object.

As there's a lot to do, let's add a subroutine to the schema (in `lib/ChatStat/Schema.pm`) called "record", which will insert an Action object into the database as follows:

```
sub record {
    my $self   = shift;
    my $action = shift;
    my $nickname = $self->_get_nickname(parse_nickname($action->who));
    my $thing    = $self->resultset('Things')->
      find_or_create({ thing => $action->word });
    my $channel  = $self->resultset('Channels')->
      find_or_create({ channel => $action->channel });
    return $self->resultset('Opinions')->
      create({ nickname => $nickname,
```

```
                    thing    => $thing,
                    points   => $action->points,
                    message  => $action->message,
                    reason   => $action->reason,
                    channel  => $channel,
                  });
}
```

All we do here is use the DBIC schema ($self) to create or find the relevant records, then we create an Opinion. We do need a _get_nickname subroutine to take the nickname (in the form of nickname!~username@hostname.com and return a nickname object that refers to a (perhaps newly-created) person object:

```
sub _get_nickname {
    my $self = shift;
    my ($nick, $user, $host) = @_;
    my $nickname = $self->resultset('Nicknames')->
      find_or_create({ nick     => $nick,
                       username => $user,
                       host     => $host,
                     });
    my $person = $nickname->person;
    if (!$person) {
        my $person = $self->resultset('People')->
          find_or_create({ name => $nick });
        $nickname->person($person);
        $nickname->update;
    }
    return $nickname;
}
```

Now we can get an Action and put it into the database with one line of code:

```
$schema->record(ChatStat::Action->new(...));
```

Let's tie this all together by creating a script in script/chatstat_add_opinion.pl so that we can add opinions from the command line as follows:

```
use strict;
use warnings;
use FindBin qw($Bin);
use lib "$Bin/../lib";
use ChatStat::Action;
use ChatStat::Schema;
my ($channel, $who, $message) = @ARGV;
```

```
die 'need channel as arg 1' unless $channel;
die 'need nickname as arg 2' unless $who;
die 'need message as arg 3' unless $message;

my $s = ChatStat::Schema->connect("DBI:SQLite:$Bin/../root/database");
die "failed to connect to database" unless $s;

my $parsed = ChatStat::Action->new($channel, $who, $message);
my $new = $s->record($parsed);

print "added opinion ". $new->oid. "\n";
```

You can now run this using the following command line:

```
$ perl script/chatstat_add_opinion.pl 'jon!~jon@jrock.us' '#foo'
'scripts++ # making my life easy'
```

**added opinion 1**

# Extracting the Data

Now that our database is full of data, it's time to make some sense out of it. We'll start by writing a function to determine the total number of points a "thing" has accumulated.

Instead of writing a script to test each query we write, we'll use a REPL (read-evaluate-print loop) to interact with our program in real time. To get a Perl REPL, install the `Devel::REPL` module from `CPAN`. That module provides a script called `re.pl`. Run `re.pl`, and you'll be able to type in Perl code as though you're at a shell prompt that understands Perl.

As an example, let us try adding an opinion from `re.pl`:

```
$ re.pl # the > is now re.pl's prompt
> use lib qw(lib);
> use ChatStat::Action;
> use ChatStat::Schema;
> my $s = ChatStat::Schema->connect('DBI:SQLite:root/database');
$ChatStat_Schema1 = ChatStat::Schema=HASH(0x8aafda0);
> my $a = ChatStat::Action->new('jon!~jon@jrock.us', '#test', '(re.
pl)++');
$ChatStat_Action1 = ChatStat::Action=HASH(0x90dbe40);
> $a->message;
(re.pl)++
> $a->reason;
> $a->points;
```

```
1
> my $o = $s->record($a);
$ChatStat_Schema_Opinions1 = ChatStat::Schema::Opinions=HASH(0x915a450);
> $o->id;
6
> $o->nickname->person->name;
jon
> exit
```

If you want to explore your program or you're only going to do something once or twice, `re.pl` is a great way to do it.

Back to the task at hand, let's write a function to return the number of points a "Thing" has accumulated. For now, we'll add this function directly to the Schema:

```
sub karma_for {
    my $schema = shift;
    my $thing  = shift;

    my $col =
      $schema->resultset('Opinions')->
        search({ 'thing.thing' => lc $thing,
               },
               {  join         => ['thing'],
               })->get_column('points');

    return $col->sum || 0;
}
```

We're introducing a few new features of `DBIx::Class` here. We start with a straightforward search of the opinions table, looking for rows where `thing.thing` equals the `$thing` passed into the function. However, there is no column called `thing.thing` in the opinions table. To get that, we want to join along the "thing" relationship we created earlier. This is what the second argument *search* does; we pass a list of relationships to join in as "join", and now the columns in the related table are available to use in the search query. (If you want to get back the value of a joined in column, specify `include_columns => [qw/table.list table.of table.columns/]` after join.)

At this point, we have a resultset. When we call `get_column` on that resultset, an object representing a single column of the resultset is returned. The object has methods like `sum` to return the sum of everything in that column, `all` to return an array of values, etc. We call `sum` to sum up the points, and then return that sum.

The critical thing to keep in mind is that even though we call methods and create objects, no query goes out to the database until we ask for a result. This means that `get_column` isn't actually getting the column from the database and converting it to a Perl array; it merely sets a flag saying *we only need to get this column when we actually run the query*. When we say `$col->sum` at the end, that tells `DBIx::Class` to execute the query; the sum command is done on the database side with the SQL function `SUM`.

We can explore the actual SQL that this command generates by setting the environment variable `DBIC_TRACE=1` and then running `karma_for`:

```
$ DBIC_TRACE=1 re.pl
> use  ...; # see above
> $s = ChatStat::Schema->connect(...); # same as last time
> $s->karma_for('catalyst');
SELECT SUM( points ) FROM opinions me  JOIN things thing ON ( thing.tid =
me.tid ) WHERE ( thing.thing = ? ): 'catalyst'
2
> exit
```

You can see that the generated SQL is pretty efficient and probably what you would have written yourself.

Let's take the `karma_for` subroutine a bit further and add an option to only count the karma that goes in a certain direction (the sum of all upvotes, the sum of all downvotes, etc).

To do this, we just need to add another condition to the search (limiting the selection to rows where points are less than zero, greater than zero, etc.). We add this to the top of `karma_for`:

```
    my $dir    = shift;

    my @points;
    if (defined $dir && $dir == -1) {
        @points = ('points' => {'<=', -1});
    }
    elsif (defined $dir && $dir == 1) {
        @points = ('points' => {'>=', 1});
    }
    elsif (defined $dir && $dir == 0) {
        @points = ('points' => {'==', 0});
    }
```

Then we pass `@points` to search:

```
search({ 'thing.thing' => lc $thing,
         @points,
       }, ...
```

Finally, if `$dir` was passed in, we will want to call the `COUNT` function instead of the `SUM` function, so we add a conditional for that before we return the sum:

```
if (defined $dir) {
    return $col->func('count');
}
```

Back in `re.pl`, we can try out the new functionality:

```
> $s->karma_for('catalyst', -1);
SELECT COUNT( points ) FROM opinions me  JOIN things thing ON ( thing.tid
= me.tid ) WHERE ( points <= ? AND thing.thing = ? ): '-1', 'catalyst'
0
> $s->karma_for('catalyst');
SELECT SUM( points ) FROM opinions me  JOIN things thing ON ( thing.tid =
me.tid ) WHERE ( thing.thing = ? ): 'catalyst'
2
>
```

# Chained ResultSets

The most powerful abstraction `DBIx::Class` provides is the ResultSet. Every query you create with `DBIx::Class` is a ResultSet, and a new ResultSet can be created by chaining a ResultSet command off of an existing ResultSet. As an example, let's use `re.pl` (and ResultSet chaining) to find a list of people that have shared their opinions on the same things I have. Let us add some sample data as follows:

```
> $s->resultset('Opinions')->delete; # clear out opinions
> $s->record(ChatStat::Action->new('jon!~a@a','a','test++'))
> $s->record(ChatStat::Action->new('jon!~a@b','a','perl++'))
> $s->record(ChatStat::Action->new('foo!~c@c','c','test++'))
> $s->record(ChatStat::Action->new('bar!~d@d','c','test--'))
> $s->record(ChatStat::Action->new('quux!~q@q','q','foobar++'))
```

Now, we'll find `jon`:

```
> my $me = $s->resultset('People')->find('jon', { key => 'nickname' })
> $me->name
jon
```

And the nicknames he's used:

```
> $me->nicknames
$ARRAY1 = [ ... ];
> map { $_->host } $me->nicknames
$ARRAY1 = ['a', 'b'];
```

This tells us that `jon` has used IRC from hosts `a` and `b`, which is exactly what we typed above.

Now, let's find opinions that those nicknames have authored:

```
> my $opinions = $me->nicknames->search_related('opinions')
> map { $_->oid } $opinions->all
$ARRAY1 = [1, 2]
```

Now we can join in the things that these opinions refer to using the following command line:

```
> my $things = $opinions->search_related('thing');
> $things->get_column('thing')->all
$ARRAY1 = [ 'test', 'perl' ];
```

Now for the fun part—we join everything back in reverse. We get the opinions that refer to these things, then we join in the nicknames that authored those opinions, then we find the person that those nicknames belong to:

```
> $things->search_related('opinions')
  ->search_related('nickname')
  ->search_related('person', {}, {group_by => 'person.name'})
  ->get_column('name')->all;
$ARRAY1 = [ 'bar', 'foo', 'jon' ];
```

To avoid duplicates at the last step, we added a `GROUP BY` clause to the query so that we would only see a person's name once.

Let's take this one step further and only show people who upmodded things that `jon` had an opinion about:

```
> $things->search_related('opinions',{'opinions_2.points'=>
                                                    {'>', 0}})
  ->search_related('nickname')
  ->search_related('person', {}, {group_by => 'person.name'})
  ->get_column('name')->all;
$ARRAY1 = [ 'foo', 'jon' ];
```

In this final query, `bar` went away because he only downmodded `test`, and that opinion was filtered out by the search passed to the first `search_related` call. Note that if a table is visited twice along the chain, it's referred to the second time by `<tablename>_2` instead of just the table name. (This scales as high as you'd like it to.)

If you're curious, the final generated SQL statement was as follows:

```
SELECT name FROM nicknames me LEFT JOIN opinions opinions ON (
opinions.nid = me.nid )  JOIN things thing ON ( thing.tid = opinions.
tid ) LEFT JOIN opinions opinions_2 ON ( opinions_2.tid = thing.tid
)  JOIN nicknames nickname ON ( nickname.nid = opinions_2.nid )  JOIN
people person ON ( person.pid = nickname.pid ) WHERE ( ( ( opinions_
2.points >= ? ) AND ( me.pid = ? ) ) ) GROUP BY person.name
```

As you can see, even though we stored intermediate results to named variables, the final query is only run once and no filtering of the results is done in Perl. Due to this, even complicated queries don't take a speed hit; they run the same as if you had executed the SQL yourself.

One last thing to note is that you need not end the chained ResultSets with `get_column` or `all`; you can use any method you would use on a normal resultset (including another `search`).

# Custom ResultSets

As the complexity of your queries increase, you might want to start giving them names so that you can use them like the other ResultSet methods. `DBIC` provides a few ways to do this. The first is to create a subclass of `DBIx::Class::ResultSet`, add a method that accepts a resultset and returns another one, and to refer to it in your Schema class:

```
__PACKAGE__->resultset_class('MyApp::ResultSet::Foo');
```

If you just want to add a few custom resultset methods throughout your application, you can use the `ResultSetManager` plug-in. This plug-in will allow you to write ResultSet methods directly inside the Schema class:

```
__PACKAGE__->load_components("ResultSetManager", "Core");
...
sub my_search :ResultSet {
  my $rs = shift;
  ...
  return $rs->...
}
```

Let's familiarize ourselves with this concept by creating a ResultSet method in the `People` class that will return similar people (by using the algorithm from the previous example).

In `People.pm`, be sure to load the `ResultSetManager` plugin as follows:

```
__PACKAGE__->load_components(
   "ResultSetManager", "PK::Auto", "Core"
);
```

Then, we just write the `similar_people` method in the following manner:

```
sub similar_people :ResultSet {
  my $rs = shift;
  return $rs
  ->search_related('nicknames')
  ->search_related('opinions')
  ->search_related('thing')
  ->search_related('opinions')
  ->search_related('nickname')
 ->search_related('person', {}, {group_by => 'person.name'});
}
```

Now we can use the `similar_people` as a ResultSet method:

```
my @similar = $people->search(...)->similar_people
                         ->get_column('names')->all;
```

Note that if you don't intend to call the method on a ResultSet (but rather a single Row in the ResultSet), then you don't need to add the `:ResultSet` tag. The normal accessors methods that are created in a Schema class may return resultsets, but they won't be called from a ResultSet. So, if you want `similar_people` to work on the result of `$people->find(...)`, you should omit the `:ResultSet` attribute from the method.

# Putting the Data on the Web

Now that we have the fundamentals of the database setup, we're ready to build a web interface. The general idea will be to present a summary of the data we collect and provide links for getting more information.

The main page, pictured below, is where we'll start. It displays the results of two queries (*highest/lowest* score and *most/least* controversial). The items themselves are links to pages that show the reasons each voter provided for upvoting or downvoting the `thing`.

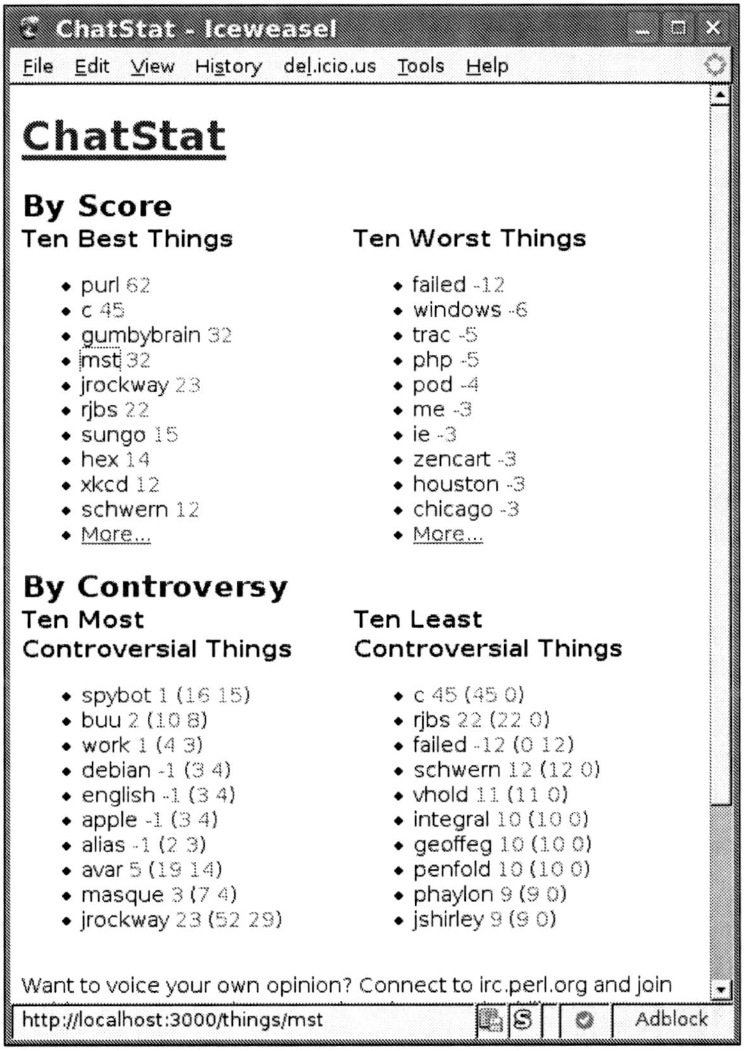

We'll start with the template work. The generic wrapper, `root/wrapper.tt2`:

```
<?xml version="1.0" encoding="utf-8"?>
<!DOCTYPE html PUBLIC "-//W3C//DTD XHTML 1.1//EN"
                      "http://www.w3.org/TR/xhtml11/DTD/xhtml11.dtd">
<html xmlns="http://www.w3.org/1999/xhtml" xml:lang="en">
  <head>
    <title>[% title || c.config.name %]</title>
    <link rel="stylesheet"
          href="[% c.uri_for('/static/main.css') %]"
          type="text/css" />
  </head>
  <body>
    <h1>
      <a href="[% c.uri_for('/') | html %]">ChatStat</a>
    </h1>
    [% content %]
    <div id="logos">
      <a href="http://www.catalystframework.org/">
        <img src="[% base %]static/btn_120x50_built.png"
             alt="Built with Catalyst" />
      </a>
    </div>
  </body>
</html>
```

With that out of the way, we can create some macros that will make writing the actual pages much easier. Every time we see a "thing", we want it to be a link to the things page. Similarly, we always want negative scores to show up in *red*, and positive scores in *green*. Finally, we want nicknames to be linked to that person's information people. To make this easy to achieve, we'll write some common macros and include those on each page. Then we can use syntax like `[% score(some_score) %]` to format our data consistently.

The macros for score, thing and person can be placed in `root/thing_macros.tt2`, and should look like the following:

```
[% # format a thing %]
[% MACRO thing(thing) BLOCK %]
<a class="thing"
   href="[% c.uri_for('/things',thing) | html%]">
  [% thing | html %]</a>
[% END %]
[% # format a person's nickname %]
[% MACRO person(person) BLOCK %]
```

```
<a class="person"
   href="[% c.uri_for('/people',person) | html%]">
  [% person | html %]</a>
[% END %]

[% # format a score %]
[% MACRO score(score) BLOCK %]
  [% IF score > 0 %]
    [% SET class = "positive" %]
  [% ELSE %]
    [% SET class = "negative" %]
  [% END %]
<span class="[% class %]_score">
[% score | html %]
</span>
[% END %]
```

As the main design element of our application is side-by-side pairs, it makes sense to create a reusable template for displaying two elements side-by-side. We'll do this by creating a template called `pair.tt2`, and including it where we need it. The code for `root/pair.tt2` looks like the following:

```
<div class="pair clearfix" [% IF width %] style="width: [% width %]"
[% END %]>
  <h2>[% title | html %]</h2>
  <div class="box left">
    <h3>[% left_title | html %]</h3>
    [% left %]
  </div>
  <div class="box right">
    <h3>[% right_title | html %]</h3>
    [% right %]
  </div>
  <br class="clear" />
</div>
```

We can use this elsewhere like the following:

```
[% INCLUDE pair.tt2
   title='Pair Title'
     left_title = 'The left side'
       left = 'some HTML for the left side'
     right_title = 'Ten right side'
       right = 'some HTML for the right side
%]
```

Before we write the main page, we just need a macro that will format a list of the thing-score tuples from the database into HTML, to pass to `pair.tt2` as left and right. As we will use this on more than just the main page, we'll put the macro in `thing_macros.tt2` with the other macros:

```
[% # transform a list of [thing, score] tuples into HTML %]
[% MACRO list_things(key,more) BLOCK %]
<ul>
  [% FOREACH row = key %]
  <li>
    [% thing(row.thing) %]
    [% score(row.total_points) %]
  </li>
  [% END %]
  [% IF more %]
  <li><a href="[% more | html %]">More...</a></li>
  [% END %]
</ul>
[% END %]
```

Now we're ready to write the main page, `root/index.tt2`.

```
[% WRAPPER wrapper.tt2  %]
[% PROCESS thing_macros.tt2 %]
[% MACRO list_controversy(rs) BLOCK %]
<ul>
[% FOREACH row IN rs %]
<li>[% thing(row.thing) %] [% score(row.total_points) %]
 (<span class="positive_score">[% row.ups | html%]</span>
  <span class="negative_score">[% row.downs | html %]</span>)
</li>
[% END %]
</ul>
[% END %]
[% INCLUDE pair.tt2
   title='By Score'
     left_title = 'Ten Best Things'
       left = list_things(top_ten,c.uri_for('/things'))
     right_title = 'Ten Worst Things'
       right = list_things(bottom_ten,c.uri_for('/things'))
%]
[% INCLUDE pair.tt2
   title='By Controversy'
     left_title = 'Ten Most Controversial Things'
       left = list_controversy(most_controversial)
```

```
      right_title = 'Ten Least Controversial Things'
        right = list_controversy(least_controversial)
%]
<p>Want to voice your own opinion?  Connect to irc.perl.org and join
[% channels | html %].  From there, just talk normally and ChatStat
will learn what you think!  </p>
[% END %]
```

We start by wrapping the page in our main wrapper. Then we include the macros. We use `PROCESS` instead of `INCLUDE` so that the macros are treated as thought they were actually typed inside `main.tt2`. (`INCLUDE` will throw them away after the included template is processed.) We continue by defining a macro to format the controversy data, since it differs slightly from the *best/worst* data. After that we're ready to show our two pairs (*best/worst* and the *controversy*), and a bit of explanatory text.

Now we need to actually get this data from the database into the template. We'll start with the root Controller in `lib/ChatStat/Controller/Root.pm`:

```
package ChatStat::Controller::Root;
use strict;
use warnings;
use base 'Catalyst::Controller';
__PACKAGE__->config(namespace => q{});
sub main : Path Args(0) {
    my ($self, $c, @args) = @_;
    $c->stash(template => 'index.tt2');
    # highest/lowest by score
    $c->stash(top_ten  => [$c->model('DBIC::Things')->highest_rated]);
    $c->stash(bottom_ten=>[$c->model('DBIC::Things')->lowest_rated ]);
    # controversy
    $c->stash(most_controversial =>
              [$c->model('DBIC::Things')->most_controversial]);
    $c->stash(least_controversial =>
              [$c->model('DBIC::Things')->least_controversial]);
    # list of joined channels
    my @channels = @{$c->config->{bot}{channels}||[]};
    my $last     = pop @channels if @channels > 1;
    my $channels = join ', ', @channels;
    $channels .= " or $last" if $last;
    $c->stash(channels  => $channels);
}
```

All we do here is call into some custom ResultSets (`highest_rated`, `lowest_rated`, `most_controversial` and `least_controversial`) that we will define in `ChatStat::Schema::Things`. We also get a list of IRC channels from the `config` file, and join those so that users looking at the page know where to go to vote for things.

The final step is to write those custom ResultSets as follows:

```
=head2 highest_rated([$how_many [, $multiplier]])

Returns a resultset page of C<$how_many> highest rated items, or 10 if
not specified.  If C<$multiplier> is C<-1>, then the lowest-rated
items are returned instead.  (C<$multiplier> defaults to 1.)

   my @top_ten = $schema->resultset('Opinions')->highest_rated();
   my @bot_ten = $schema->resultset('Opinions')->highest_rated(10, -1);
   my @top_40  = $schema->resultset('Opinions')->highest_rated(40);
   ...

From there:

   my $first = @top_ten[0];
   say $first->thing->thing. ' has '. $first->total_points. ' points';

=cut

sub highest_rated :ResultSet {
    my $self  = shift;
    my $count = shift || 10;
    my $mult  = shift || 1;

    croak "bad multiplier $mult; use 1 or -1"
      if $mult != -1 && $mult != 1;

    my $sort = $mult > 0 ? 'DESC' : 'ASC';
    return $self->search({},
                         { '+select' => [{ SUM => 'opinions.points'}],
                           '+as'     => [qw/total_points/],
                           join      => ['opinions'],
                           group_by  => 'me.tid',
                           order_by  => "SUM(opinions.points) $sort",
                           rows      => $count,
                           page      => 1,
                         });
}

=head2 lowest_rated([$how_many])

Abbreviation for highest_rated($how_many, -1)

=cut

sub lowest_rated :ResultSet {
    shift->highest_rated(shift(), -1);
}
```

lowest_rated is just an alias for highest_rated, but sorted backwards. highest_rated is where all of the real work happens. The top part of the function reads the arguments and translates 1 or -1 into DESC or ASC sort order and supplies values for optional arguments. The real meat is the call to search. The empty {} passed means that we don't want to constrain the results at all; we want every row in the Things table. The next hashref is a list of modifiers. +select says to select additional columns, specified as an array reference. Here we're selecting SUM(opinions.points). We can use "opinions" as we passed it as an argument to the join attribute. Note that "opinions" is the name of the DBIx::Class relationship, not the name of the table. The +as we pass gives the SUM(opinions.points) a name, total_points, that we can pass to get_column to get the value. For convenience, we should create an accessor to get this for us:

```
sub total_points {
    my $self = shift;
    # if we've joined this in, use the version we already have
    my $fast = eval { $self->get_column('total_points') };
    return $fast if defined $fast;
    # if it's not there, compute it with another SQL query
    return $self->opinions->get_column('points')->sum;
}
```

This accessor first looks to see if we already have total_points, and if we do, returns it. If we don't ask for total_points when we do the query, it will be calculated separately. (Note that if you're going to call total_points on every row, it's best to join it in like we do in highest_rated. If you don't, every call will result in a trip to the database, requiring a new query for every single row.)

We have seen the other attributes passed to search in the highest_rated string. order_by defines the sort order (like SQL's ORDER BY keyword) and group_by will set the grouping for aggregates, in this case the tid column in opinions. Rows and page set up paging; we usually want 10 rows and the first page, so we pass 10 and 1 to each of those attributes.

With that in place, the first half of our main page loads. Now we just need the controversy data. Here are least_controversial and most_controversial:

```
sub most_controversial :ResultSet {
    my $self  = shift;
    my $count = shift;
    my $algo = '-(ABS(SUM(points))+COUNT(1))/(COUNT(1)+0.1)';
    $self->_controversial($count, $algo, 'DESC');
}
sub least_controversial :ResultSet {
```

```
        my $self  = shift;
        my $count = shift;
        my $algo = '-ABS(SUM(points))/(COUNT(1)+0.8)';
        $self->_controversial($count, $algo, 'ASC');
    }
```

These methods simply set up the SQL for determining the controversy and pass it to the `_controversial` function, which does the real work. For the curious, I fine-tuned the controversy algorithm by writing a small REPL (included in the `contrib` directory of the source code) this accepts a SQL statement (`$algo` above) and shows the top 10 rows sorted by the result of that query. This allowed me to tweak the algorithm with real data until I liked the result. (The basic idea is that the most controversial items have scores close to zero because they've been upmodded and downmodded an equal number of times. The least controversial items have high scores with little opposition.)

Here's `_controversial`, which does the real work:

```
    sub _controversial :ResultSet {
        my $self  = shift;
        my $count = shift || 10;
        my $algo  = shift;
        my $order = shift;

        $algo .= ' co';

        return
          $self->search({},
                        { '+select' => [ \$algo,
                                         { SUM => 'points'},
                                         \'ABS(SUM((POINTS+1)/2))',
                                         \'ABS(SUM((POINTS-1)/2))',
                                         { COUNT => 1 },
                                       ],
                    '+as'     => [qw/controversy total_points ups downs c/],
                          join      => ['opinions'],
                          group_by  => 'me.tid',
                          order_by  => "co $order",
                          having    => "COUNT(1) > 5",
                          rows      => $count,
                          page      => 1,
                        });
    }
```

What we do here is to select the controversy rating (`$algo`), the total score, the number of upmods, the number of downmods, and the total count of upmods and downmods (for ordering). We introduce a new attribute here, having, which is the same as SQL's `HAVING` clause.

Now we have everything we need to run the application. If you start the app, you should be able to visit the main page and see the highest rated things, lowest rated things, most controversial things, and least controversial things. All that's missing is formatting, which you can get by creating a `root/static/main.css`, which looks like the following:

```
* {
    background-color: white;
}
h2 { margin: 0 }
span.positive_score {
    color: green;
}
span.negative_score {
    color: red;
}
a.thing {
    color: black;
    text-decoration: none;
}
.pair {
    width: 30em;
}
.pair h3 {
    margin: 0;
    padding: 0;
}
.box   {
    width: 47%;
}
.pair .left  {
    float: left;
}
.pair .right {
    float: right;
}
.clearfix:after {
    content: ".";
    display: block;
```

```
        height: 0px;
        clear: both;
        visibility: hidden;
    }
    #logos {
        padding-top: 2em;
    }
    #logos img {
        border: none;
    }
```

Now you can reload and see everything neatly laid out (and with pretty colors).

At this point, we're ready to start making some of the links work. We'll start with the `more...` link, which shows a list of everything in the database.

Let's start by adding a ResultSet that will return everything and its score to `lib/ChatStat/Schema/Things.pm`:

```
sub everything :ResultSet {
    my $self  = shift;
    return $self->search({},
                         { '+select' => { SUM =>
                                            'opinions.points' },
                           '+as'     => 'total_points',
                           join      => 'opinions',
                           group_by  => 'opinions.tid',
                         });
```

This is simple compared to the queries we wrote before. We're simply selecting everything and adding the total points to the results.

> This query is actually a superset of the queries we wrote above. As ResultSets can be chained, it's possible to write the other queries as a search chained off of this one. The code size is about the same, though, so I chose to do all three separately.

With this `everything` query, let's move on to writing the Controller. We'll need to create a new one, `lib/ChatStat/Controller/Things.pm`, and add the following:

```
package ChatStat::Controller::Things;
use strict;
use warnings;
use base 'Catalyst::Controller';
```

```
sub all_things :Path Args(0) {
    my ($self, $c) = @_;
    $c->stash(template   => 'things.tt2');
    $c->stash(everything => [
        $c->model('DBIC::Things')->
             everything->search({},{ order_by =>
                                   'SUM(opinions.points) DESC'})
                               ]);
}
1;
```

Here we get a list of everything with our `everything` ResultSet method, and then filter it further, so it's sorted according to the number of points.

Finally, we need a template, `root/things.tt2`, to display this data:

```
[% WRAPPER wrapper.tt2 %]
<h2>Every Thing</h2>
[% PROCESS thing_macros.tt2 %]
[% FOREACH row = everything %]
<p>[% thing(row.thing) %] [% score(row.total_points) %]</p>
[% END %]
[% END %]
```

Writing the template becomes pretty simple when all the macros are set up for you in advance.

Now we're ready to write the most interesting page in the application, the "thing" overview page. On this page, we'll be able to see the karma for the item, the number of upmods and downmods, and all of the written opinions. Here's what the page will look like:

As we already have most of the data we need for this page, let's start by writing the controller. Below the `all_things` method we just wrote, add a `one_thing` method:

```
sub one_thing :Path Args(1) {
    my ($self, $c, $thing) = @_;
    my $m = $c->model('DBIC');
    # aggregates
    $c->stash(template => 'thing.tt2');
    $c->stash(thing    => $thing);
    $c->stash(points   => $m->karma_for($thing));
    $c->stash(ups      => $m->karma_for($thing, 1));
    $c->stash(downs    => $m->karma_for($thing, -1));
    $c->stash(person   => $m->resultset('People')->
              find({ name => $thing}, { key => 'nickname' })
             );
    # detailed reasons
    my @reasons = $c->model('DBIC::Things')->reasons_for($thing);
    my @up_r = grep { $_->points >  0 } @reasons;
    my @dn_r = grep { $_->points <  0 } @reasons;
    my @nu_r = grep { $_->points == 0 } @reasons;
    $c->stash(up_reasons      => \@up_r);
    $c->stash(down_reasons    => \@dn_r);
    $c->stash(neutral_reasons => \@nu_r);
}
```

Note that this action accepts one argument (the thing), so that it is `:Path Args(1)` instead of `:Path Args(0)`.

We do have a few queries in this action. We get the karma for the thing, and the number of ups and downs it received. We also look for a person with the same nickname as the thing and pass it to the template if there is one. Finally, we get all the textual reasons for this `things`, and sort them into upmod reasons, downmod reasons, and neutral reasons.

Here's the code (in `Schema::Things`) for `reasons_for`:

```
sub reasons_for :ResultSet {
    my $self   = shift;
    my $thing  = shift;

    return $self->
      search({ thing => $thing })->
        search_related(opinions => {reason => {'<>' => q{}}});
}
```

This method returns all the opinions that are related to this thing, that have a non-NULL (or empty) textual reason.

The template for this action, `root/thing.tt2`, is straightforward as follows:

```
[% WRAPPER wrapper.tt2 %]
[% PROCESS thing_macros.tt2 %]
[% MACRO list_reasons(opinions) BLOCK %]
  [% FOREACH opinion = opinions %]
  <div class="reason">
   <p><span class="opinion_reason">[% opinion.reason | html %]</span>
     <span class="written_by">[% person(opinion.person) %]</span>
   </p>
  </div>
  [% END %]
  [% IF opinions.size < 1 %] <p>None!</p> [% END %]
[% END %]

<h2>Information on [% c.stash.thing | html %]</h2>
<p>[% c.stash.thing | html %] has karma of [% score(points) %] from
being upmodded [% score(ups) %] times and downmodded
<span class="negative_score">[% downs | html %]</span> times.
</p>

[% IF c.stash.person %]
<p>[% person(c.stash.thing) %] is also a person!</p>
[% END %]

[% INCLUDE pair.tt2
   left_title  = "Reasons why " _ c.stash.thing _ " is loved"
   right_title = "Reasons why " _ c.stash.thing _ " is hated"
   left  = list_reasons(up_reasons)
   right = list_reasons(down_reasons)
   width = "50em"
%]

<div class="pair" style="width: 50em">
<div class="box" style="padding-left: 13em; padding-right: 13em;">
[% IF neutral_reasons.size > 0 %]
<h3>Reasons why [% c.stash.thing | html %] is meh</h3>
[% list_reasons(neutral_reasons) %]
[% END %]
</div>
</div>

[% END %]
```

We include our usual macros and then define one to format the *up/down/neutral* reasons into HTML. Then we start the actual body of the page, which is a bit of text showing the upmod and downmod count, and then a pair of reason lists. If we find a person that has the same name as `thing`, we display a link to that page. Below the pair of reason lists, we display the neutral reasons if there are any.

The final thing we need to do is to give each person a page, so that the `person()` links we create everywhere actually work. This page will show a list of the user's favorite and least favorite things and a list of machines that he has used.

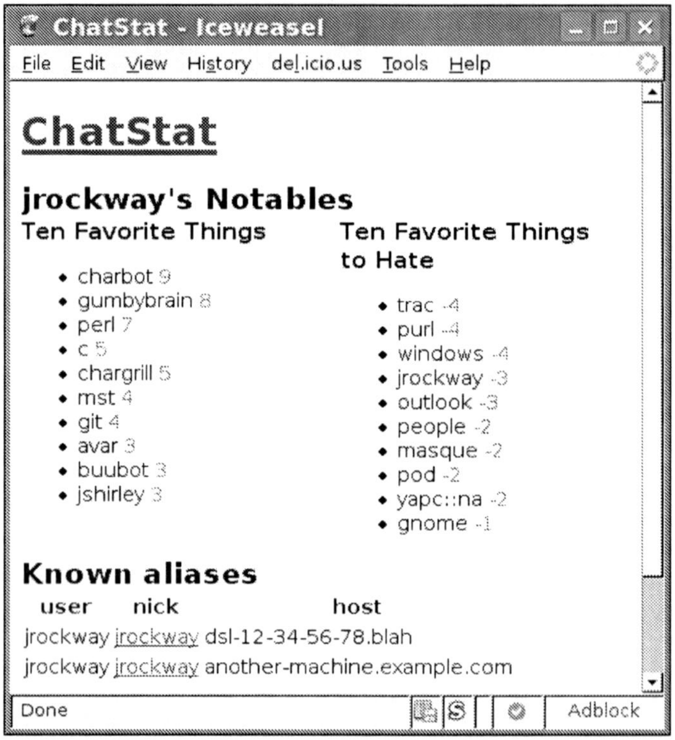


The controller, `People.pm`, will look like the following:

```
package ChatStat::Controller::People;
use strict;
use warnings;
use base 'Catalyst::Controller::BindLex';
sub one_person :Path :Args(1) {
    my ($self, $c, $name) = @_;
    $c->stash(template => 'person.tt2');
```

```
    # find who we're looking for
    my $person :Stashed = $c->model('DBIC::People')->
      find($name, {key => 'nickname'});

    $c->detach('/error_404', [qq{No such person "$name"}]) unless
$person;

    # get nicknames
    my $nicknames :Stashed = $person->nicknames;
    my $nickids = [$nicknames->get_column('nid')->all];
    my @cond    = ( { 'opinions.nid' =>
                        { -in => $nickids },
                      },
                      { join => 'opinions' }
                    );

    # and do the search for things' scores
    my $t = $c->model('DBIC::Things');
    my @high :Stashed = $t->highest_rated->search(@cond);
    my @low  :Stashed = $t->lowest_rated->search(@cond);
}
1;
```

We start by finding the requested `person`, and detaching to a `404` page if it doesn't exist. The code for the `404` page is in `Root.pm`:

```
sub error_404 :Private {
    my ($self, $c, $reason) = @_;
    $reason ||= 'Not found';
    $c->stash(reason   => $reason);
    $c->stash(template => '404.tt2');
    $c->response->status(404);
}
```

And the template, `root/404.tt2`:

```
[% WRAPPER wrapper.tt2 %]
<h2>404 Not Found</h2>
<p>[% reason | html %]</p>
<a href="[% c.uri_for('/') %]">Go home</a>?
[% END %]
```

After we have a Person, we get a list of the nickname IDs that he has used, and use that data to build up some constraints that will limit a query of opinions to ones by that user. Finally, we use our `highest_rated` and `lowest_rated` ResultSets to get the highest and lowest rated items, but with a twist—we search within that ResultSet and limit it to the nicknames used by the requested Person. In this way, we get a top and bottom ten list for a specific user.

Once we have the data, we just need to show it via `root/person.tt2`:

```
[% WRAPPER wrapper.tt2 %]
[% PROCESS thing_macros.tt2 %]
[% INCLUDE pair.tt2
   title= c.stash.person.name _ "'s Notables"
     left_title = 'Ten Favorite Things'
       left = list_things(high)
     right_title = 'Ten Favorite Things to Hate'
       right = list_things(low)
%]
<h2>Known aliases</h2>
<table>
<tr><th>user</th><th>nick</th><th>host</th></tr>
[% WHILE (nick = nicknames.next) %]
<tr>
  <td>[% nick.username | html %]</td>
  <td>[% person(nick.nick)    %]</td>
  <td>[% nick.host      | html %]</td>
</tr>
[% END %]
</table>
[% END %]
```

Here, we reuse the `list_things` macro we wrote for the main page and show the pair of *best/worst* things. Then we use the `Person` object to display some information about the nicknames that person has used.

For completeness, let's also add an action for displaying a list of all people:

```
sub everyone :Path Args(0) {
    my ($self, $c) = @_;
    my $people :Stashed = $c->model('DBIC::People');
    $c->stash(template => 'people.tt2');
}
```

The template is simple:

```
[% WRAPPER wrapper.tt2 %]
[% PROCESS thing_macros.tt2 %]
<h2>Everyone</h2>
<ul>
[% WHILE (the_person = people.next) %]
<li>[% person(the_person.name) %]</li>
[% END %]
</ul>
[% END %]
```

That's all we need for the read-only part of the interface. Everything that's linked to it works.

Let us add one last feature to the Things controller to demonstrate Catalyst's Chained dispatch type. We'll provide two additional actions, "ups" and "downs" to get just a list of up reasons and down reasons for each thing. The URL will look like /things/<the thing>/ups and /things/<the thing>/downs.

Without the Chained dispatch type, writing something like this would be ugly. You would have to get the second argument (if there was one), figure out whether it was up or down, then do something based on that information. Chained makes this sort of thing trivial.

To get started, we'll modify the existing actions a bit. Instead of:

```
sub one_thing :Path Args(1) { ... }
```

We'll start a Chain as follows:

```
sub thing_setup :Chained('/') PathPart('things') CaptureArgs(1) {
    my ($self, $c, $thing) = @_;
    $c->stash(thing => $thing);
    my $m = $c->model('DBIC');

    # rest of the action, except setting the template
}
```

This will start a chain that will capture one argument whenever /things/* is hit. The argument to Chained is usually the chain that your action applies to, but to start a chain you attach it to /. PathPart is what URL part you want after the chain (things after /) in this case. CaptureArgs will take a number of arguments off the URL and pass them to the action before trying to match the rest of the chain.

This won't do anything itself; chains need an endpoint. So, we'll add one_thing endpoint to restore the functionality that we had before:

```
sub one_thing :Chained('thing_setup') PathPart('') Args(0) {
    my ($self, $c) = @_;
    $c->stash(template => 'thing.tt2');
}
```

Here we're chaining this endpoint of thing_setup with an empty name, and accepting no arguments. Note that in the middle of the chain you say CaptureArgs, but at an endpoint you just say Args as usual.

Now the old action will work like it did before. However, adding new actions that operate on a thing is quite easy:

```
sub ups :Chained('thing_setup') Args(0) {
    my ($self, $c) = @_;
    $c->stash(template => 'reasons_simple.tt2');
    $c->stash(things => $c->stash->{up_reasons});
}
sub downs :Chained('thing_setup') Args(0) {
    my ($self, $c) = @_;
    $c->stash(template => 'reasons_simple.tt2');
    $c->stash(things => $c->stash->{down_reasons});
}
```

In this case we can omit `PathPart`, because it defaults to the name of the action, and that's what we want this time.

That's all we need to do to add actions that only show ups or downs on the page. The setup work happens in `thing_setup`, and the endpoints that chain off that do the minimum amount of work needed to show the page.

To see this in action, just create the template, `root/reasons_simple.tt2`:

```
<html>
<title>Reasons for [% thing | html %]</title>
<body>
<ul>
[% FOREACH thing = things %]
<li>[% thing.reason | html %]</li>
[% END %]
</ul>
</body>
</html>
```

Adding a `/ups` or `/downs` off any thing's page's URL will now show the simple list of reasons for that thing.

Note that you can chain chains from chains, so that you aren't limited to a URL like `/base/<argument>/endpoint`. You can chain as many times as you like, so `/base/<argument>/something/<argument>/endpoint` is perfectly legal (and useful).

# Summary

In this chapter, we created a new application called `ChatStat`. As it's database heavy, we took a look at the features of `DBIC` that make handling all the data easy. We then used Catalyst to get the data from `DBIC` and onto the web. We saw the value of putting data logic into the Model (in the form of custom accessors and ResultSets), and how Catalyst's chained dispatcher makes it easy to add actions onto other actions.

# 6
# Building Your Own Model

In the last few chapters, we've seen how `DBIx::Class` can provide a powerful interface to your data. Sometimes, however, `DBIx::Class` is not the right tool for the job. Situations often arise in which your application won't be able to access database tables directly and instead you'll need to access data through predefined stored procedures. In this case, `DBIx::Class` would be useless as you aren't able to read and modify objects with the usual `SELECT`, `INSERT`, `UPDATE`, and `DELETE` command set—everything must be done by calling a procedure and reading back the result.

In other cases, your data won't be in a database at all. You might instead choose to store and retrieve information from files in a directory.

In this chapter, we'll cover three common cases—mixing a procedural interface with a relational `DBIx::Class` interface, writing a database interface without `DBIx::Class`, and building a custom Model that doesn't use a database at all.

## Extending a DBIx::Class Model

A common occurrence is a situation in which your application has free reign over most of the database, but needs to use a few stored procedure calls to get at certain pieces of data. In that case, you'll want to create a normal DBIC schema and then add methods for accessing the unusual data.

As an example, let's look back to the `AddressBook` application and imagine that for some reason we couldn't use `DBIx::Class` to access the user table, and instead need to write the raw SQL to return an array containing everyone's username. In `AddressBook::Model::AddressDB`, we just need to write a subroutine to do our work as follows:

```
package AddressBook::Model::AddressDB;
// other code in the package
sub get_users {
```

```
        my $self = shift;
        my $storage = $self->storage;
        return $storage->dbh_do(
          sub {
            my $self = shift;
            my $dbh  = shift;
            my $sth = $dbh->prepare('SELECT username FROM user');
            $sth->execute();
            my @rows = @{$sth->fetchall_arrayref()};
            return map { $_->[0] } @rows;
            });
    }
```

Here's how the code works. On the first line, we get our `DBIC::Schema` object and then obtain the schema's `storage` object. The storage object is what DBIC uses to execute its generated SQL on the database, and is usually an instance of `DBIx::Class::Storage::DBI`. This class contains a method called `dbh_do` which will execute a piece of code, passed to `dbh_do` as a coderef (or "anonymous subroutine"), and provide the code with a standard `DBI` database handle (usually called `$dbh`). `dbh_do` will make sure that the database handle is valid before it calls your code, so you don't need to worry about things like the database connection timing out. `DBIC` will reconnect if necessary and then call your code. `dbh_do` will also handle exceptions raised within your code in a standard way, so that errors can be caught normally.

The rest of the code deals with actually executing our query. When the database handle is ready, it's passed as the second argument to our coderef (the first is the storage object itself, in case you happen to need that). Once we have the database handle, the rest of the code is exactly the same as if we were using plain `DBI` instead of `DBIx::Class`. We first prepare our query (which need not be a `SELECT`; it could be `EXEC` or *anything* else), execute it and, finally, process the result. The map statement converts the returned data to the form we expect it in, a list of names (instead of a list of rows each containing a single name). Note that the return statement in the coderef returns to `dbh_do`, not to the caller of `get_users`. This means that you can execute `dbh_do` as many times as required and then further process the results before returning from the `get_users` subroutine.

Once you've written this subroutine, you can easily call it from elsewhere in your application:

```
my @users = $c->model('AddressDB')->get_users;
$c->response->body('All Users' join ', ', @users);
```

# Custom Methods Without Raw SQL

As the above example doesn't use any features of the database that DBIC doesn't explicitly expose in its resultset interface, let us see how we can implement the get_users function without using dbh_do. Although the preconditions of the example indicated that we couldn't use DBIC, it's good to compare the two approaches so you can decide which way to do things in your application. Here's another way to implement the above example:

```
sub get_users { # version 2
    my $self = shift;
    my $users = $self->resultset('User');
    my @result;
    while(my $user = $users->next){
       push @result, $user->username;
    }
    return @result;
}
```

This looks like the usual DBIC manipulation that we're used to. (Usually we call `$c->model('AddressDB::User')` to get the "User" resultset, but under the hood this is the same as `$c->model('AddressDB')->resultset('User')`. In this example, `$self` is the same as `$c->model('AddressDB')`.)

The above code is cleaner and more portable (across database systems) than the dbh_do method, so it's best to prefer resultsets over dbh_do unless there's absolutely no other way to achieve the functionality you desire.

# Calling Database Functions

Another common problem is the need to call database functions on tables that you're accessing with DBIC. Fortunately, DBIC provides syntax for this case, so we won't need to write any SQL manually and run it with dbh_do. All that's required is a second argument to search. For example, if we want to get the count of all users in the user table, we could write (in a controller) the following:

```
$users = $c->model('AddressDB::User');
$users->search({}, { select => [ { COUNT => 'id' } ],
                         as => [ 'count'            ],});
$count = $users->first->get_column('count');
```

This is the same as executing `SELECT COUNT(id) FROM user`, fetching the first row and then setting `$count` to the first column of that row.

Note that we didn't specify a WHERE clause, but if we wanted to, we could replace the first {} with the WHERE expression, and then get the count of matching rows. Here's a function that we can place in the User ResultSetClass to get easy access to the user count:

```
sub count_users_where {
   my $self      = shift;
   my $condition = shift;
   $self->search($condition,
        { select => [ { COUNT => 'id' } ],
              as => [ 'count' ], });
   my $first = $users->first;
   return $first->get_column('count') if $first;
   return 0; # if there is no "first" row, return 0
}
```

Now, we can write something like the following:

```
$jons = $c->model('AddressDB::User')->
           count_users_where([ username => {-like => '%jon%'}]);
```

to get the number of jons in the database, without having to fetch every record and count them.

If you only need to work with a single column, you can also use the DBIx::Class::ResultSetColumn interface.

# Creating a Database Model from Scratch

In some cases, you'll have no use for any of DBIC's functionality. DBIC might not work with your database, or perhaps you're migrating a legacy application that has well-tested database queries that you don't want to rewrite. In this sort of situation, you can write the entire database model manually.

In the next example, we'll use Catalyst::Model::DBI to set up the basic DBI layer and the write methods (like we did above) to access the data in the model. As we have the AddressBook application working, we'll add a DBI model and write some queries against the AddressBook database.

First, we need to create the model. We'll call it AddressDBI:

```
$ perl script/addressbook_create.pl model AddressDBI DBI DBI:SQLite:
database
```

When you open the generated `AddressBook::Model::AddressDBI` file, you should see something like this:

```
package AddressBook::Model::AddressDBI;

use strict;
use base 'Catalyst::Model::DBI';

__PACKAGE__->config(
    dsn          => 'DBI:SQLite:database',
    user         => '',
    password     => '',
    options      => {},
);
1; # magic true value required
```

Once you have this file, you can just start adding methods. The database handle will be available via `$self->dbh`, and the rest is up to you. Let's add a `count_users` function:

```
sub count_users {
    my $self = shift;
    my $dbh  = $self->dbh;

    my $rows = $dbh->
        selectall_arrayref('SELECT COUNT(id) FROM user');
    return $rows->[0]->[0]; # first row, then the first column
}
```

Let's also add a test Controller so that we can see if this method works. First, create the Test controller by running the following command line:

```
$ perl script/addressbook_create.pl controller Test
```

And then add a quick test action as follows:

```
sub count_users : Local {
    my ($self, $c) = @_;

    my $count = $c->model('AddressDBI')->count_users();
    $c->response->body("There are $count users.");
}
```

You can quickly see the output of this action by running the following command line:

```
$ perl script/addressbook_test.pl /test/count_users
There are 2 users.
```

> The `myapp_test.pl` script will work for any action, but it works best for test actions like this because the output is plain-text and will fit on the screen. When you're testing actual actions in your application, it's usually easier to read the page when you view it in the browser.

That's all there is to it—just add methods to `AddressDBI` until you have everything you need.

The only other thing you might want to do is to add the database configuration to your `config` file, like we did in Chapter 4. It works almost the same way for `DBI` as it does for `DBIC::Schema`:

```
---
name: AddressBook
Model::AddressDBI:
  dsn: "DBI:SQLite:database"
  username: ~
  password: ~
   options:
     option1: something
     # and so on
# the rest of your config file goes here
```

# Implementing a Filesystem Model

In this final example, we'll build an entire model from scratch without even the help of a model base class like `Catalyst::Model::DBI`. Before you do this for your own application, you should check the CPAN to see if anyone's done anything similar already. There are currently about fifty ready-to-use model base classes that abstract data sources like LDAP servers, RSS readers, shopping carts, search engines, Subversion, email folders, web services and even YouTube. Expanding upon one of these classes will usually be easier than writing everything yourself.

For this example, we'll create a very simple blog application. To post the blog, you just write some text and put it in a file whose name is the title you want on the post. We'll write a filesystem model from scratch to provide the application with the blog posts.

Let's start by creating the app's skeleton:

```
$ catalyst.pl Blog
```

After that, we'll create our Filesystem model:

```
$ cd Blog
$ perl script/blog_create.pl model Filesystem
```

We'll also use plain TT for the View:

```
$ perl script/blog_create.pl view TT TT
```

Let's continue by creating a template for displaying the most recent blog posts, called `root/recent.tt`:

```
<html>
<head><title>Recent blog posts</title></head>
<body>
<h1>Blog</h1>
[% FOREACH post = posts %]
<h2>[% post.title | html %]</h2>
<i>Written on [% post.created | html %]</i>
[% post.body %]
[% END %]
</body>
</html>
```

Finally, let's replace the default index action with one that gets the posts from the model and then displays them inside the recent.tt template. In `Blog::Controller::Root`, we'll replace `default` with the following code:

```
sub default : Private {
    my ( $self, $c ) = @_;
    $c->stash->{template} = 'recent.tt';
    #$c->stash->{posts} = [$c->model('Filesystem')
    #                              ->get_recent_posts()];
}
```

Note that we've commented out the line where we get the posts, since we haven't implemented the `get_recent_posts` method yet. You should be able to start the application now and see the beginnings of a blog when you visit `http://localhost:3000/`.

All that's left to do is implement the model. This model will take a two-tiered approach. The actual Catalyst model will find all "posts" and will create a `Blog::Model::Filesystem::Post` object for each. These objects will do most of the work—reading the file, etc. Let's start by creating the Post class by writing `lib/Blog/Model/Filesystem/Post.pm`:

```
# Post.pm
package Blog::Model::Filesystem::Post;
use strict;
use warnings;
use Carp;
use File::Basename;
use File::Slurp qw(read_file);
use File::CreationTime qw(creation_time);
use base 'Class::Accessor';
__PACKAGE__->mk_ro_accessors(qw(filename));
sub new {
    my $class    = shift;
    my $filename = shift;
    croak "Must specify a filename" unless $filename;
    my $self = {};
    $self->{filename} = $filename;
    bless $self, $class;
    return $self;
}
sub title {
    my $self     = shift;
    my $filename = $self->filename;
    my $title    = basename($filename);
    $title       =~ s/[.](\w+)$//; # strip off .extensions
    return $title;
}
sub body {
    my $self = shift;
    return read_file($self->filename);
}
sub created {
    my $self = shift;
    return creation_time($self->filename);
}
sub modified {
    my $self = shift;
    return (stat $self->filename)[9]; # 9 is mtime
}
1;
```

This is a pretty standard Perl class. The new method takes a filename and creates an instance of this class based on the filename. The rest of the methods access the file and return the desired information. Because of the way we've designed the class, it will be extremely simple to add more information to each blog post in the future. We'll just create another method, and the information will be easily available to the controller and the template.

Now we need to create the actual Catalyst model that will find blog posts and return instances of the above Post object. To start with, we'll just need to add the `get_recent_posts method` in the following manner:

```
package Blog::Model::Filesystem;
use strict;
use warnings;
use base 'Catalyst::Model';
use Carp;
use File::Spec;
use Blog::Model::Filesystem::Post;
__PACKAGE__->mk_accessors('base');
sub get_recent_posts {
    my $self = shift;
    my $base = $self->base;
    my @articles;
    opendir my $dir, $base or
                                croak "Problem opening $base: $!";
    while(my $file = readdir $dir){
     next if $file =~ /^[.]/; # skip hidden files
          my $filename = File::Spec->catfile($base, $file);
          next if -d $filename;
          push @articles,
                 Blog::Model::Filesystem::Post->new($filename);
    }
    closedir $dir;
    @articles = reverse sort {$a->created <=> $b->created}

                                @articles;
    return @articles if @articles < 5;
    return @articles[0..4]; # top 5 otherwise
}
```

The mk_accessors line is especially important—this will allow you to specify a "base" attribute in the config file, which will then be available in the rest of the methods as $self->base. Here's the config file, blog.yml:

```
---
name: Blog
Model::Filesystem:
  base: /tmp/test
```

Now all you need to do is remove the comment from the line in Root.pm and then add some HTML files to /tmp/test. When you start your server, you should see the 5 most recent posts displayed!

(If you're interested in taking this idea further, check out the Angerwhale blogging system, available from the CPAN. It uses a similar filesystem-based model, but one that has many more features.)

# Tweaking the Model

With the core functionality in place, we can now dig a bit deeper into the model and add some more features. The first one is a sort of "user interface" improvement. Instead of making the user type out the Model::Filesystem part in the config file, it would be nice to just specify "base" and have that take the effect in the same way. We can achieve this by reading the value of $c->config->{base} into $c->config->{Model::Filesystem}->{base} just before Catalyst creates an instance of the class. This is done by overriding the COMPONENT method in the model. The COMPONENT method is called to setup things like configuration right before the new method is called (things like database connections are set up). We can override this in our model, tweak the config, and then call the version of COMPONENT in Catalyst::Model to finish everything up:

```
sub COMPONENT {
    my ($class, $app, $args) = @_;
    $args->{base} = $app->config->{base};
    return $class->NEXT::COMPONENT($app, $args);
}
```

> We call $c $app at this point, because $c usually means that there is a request occurring, whereas $app is just the static data that "is" your application. The current version of Catalyst lets you treat these objects the same way, but Catalyst 5.8 will distinguish between them. This will allow Catalyst applications to embed each other, among other things.

With this code in place, we can change the config file to:

```
---
base: /tmp/test
name: Blog
```

The last feature we'll add is validation of "base" in the `new` method. This will check to see if the base directory exists, and if it does not, issue an error message and prevent the application from starting:

```
sub new {
    my $class = shift;
    my  $self = $class->NEXT::new(@_); # get the real self
    my  $base = $self->base;
    croak "base $base does not exist" if !-d $base;
    return $self;
}
```

If you're inheriting from a base class, you can control whether or not your code runs before that of your base class by choosing whether to run your code before or after the `NEXT::new()` call. `NEXT::new()` is where the superclasses get a chance to set themselves up, then control is passed back to you. You should return the result of `NEXT::new()` from the new method.

# Request Context Inside the Model

Generally, your model's configuration won't change as requests run. When Catalyst is started, your model is initialized and it doesn't see the rest of your application again. This means that you can't save the `$app` you got from `COMPONENT` and use it to, say, access `$c->request` or `$c->response` in the future. It's generally a good idea to avoid touching the request from inside a model (that's what the Controller is for) anyway, but if you absolutely need to, you can get the latest `$c` by implementing an `ACCEPT_CONTEXT` method in your model. It's called by Catalyst every time you call `$c->model()` and is passed `$c` and any arguments are passed to `$c->model()`. In general, it will look something like this:

```
__PACKAGE__->mk_accessors(qw|context|); # at the top
sub ACCEPT_CONTEXT {
    my ($self, $c, @args) = @_;
    $self->context($c);
    return $self;
}
```

We return `$self` from `ACCEPT_CONTEXT` here, but in theory you can return anything. The value is passed directly back to the caller of `$c->model()`. `DBIC::Schema` takes advantage of this feature to return individual resultsets instead of the entire schema depending on how `$c->model()` is invoked.

After you've added an `ACCEPT_CONTEXT` method like the above, you can call `$self->context()` anywhere in your model to get the current request context.

# Maintainable Models

When you're writing your own data model for use with Catalyst, you might want to consider making it work without Catalyst first, and then later adding some glue to make it easy to use from within Catalyst. The advantage of this approach is that you can test your model without having to have a Catalyst app to use it and that you can use your data model class in non-Catalyst applications. `DBIx::Class` takes this approach, the `DBIx::Class::Schema` works fine without Catalyst. The `DBIC` model you create for your application is just a bit of glue to make using the `DBIx::Class::Schema` from Catalyst convenient.

Let's take a look at how we would build the `Filesystem` model in this manner. First, we'll move the `Blog::Model::Filesystem::Post` class to the `Blog::Backend::Filesystem::Post` namespace. Then, we'll write our post access code in `Blog::Backend::Filesystem` instead of `Blog::Model::Filesystem`. The code is exactly the same, except we'll write our own new method:

```
package Blog::Backend::Filesystem;
use strict;
use warnings;
use Carp;
use Blog::Backend::Filesystem::Post;
sub new {
    my ($class, $args) = @_; # args is { base => 'path' }
    croak 'need a base that exists' if !-d $args->{base};
    return bless $args, $class;
}
# then the same as Blog::Model::Filesystem above, substituting
# Blog::Backend::Filesystem::Post for
# Blog::Model::Filesystem::Post.
```

Now you have a class that you can use to access blog posts from outside of Catalyst. Just instantiate it like my `$post_model = Blog::Backend::Filesystem->new({ base => '/var/blog' })` and then use `$post_model` like you did `$c->model('Filesystem')` above.

The final step is to create the glue to bind the backend class to a Catalyst model. Fortunately, `Catalyst::Model::Adaptor`, a module on CPAN, will do that for us automatically by running the following command line:

```
$ perl script/blog_create.pl model Filesystem Adaptor Blog::Backend::
Filesystem
```

That command will create a Model called `Blog::Model::Filesystem` which simply returns a `Blog::Backend::Filesystem` object when you call `$c->model('Filesystem')`. It works by creating a subclass of `Catalyst::Model::Adaptor`, which will create an instance of your backend class at startup and return it when needed.

One disadvantage is that the configuration format changes slightly:

```
---
Model::Filesystem:
   args:
      base: /var/blog
```

If you want to avoid the unsightly `args` key, you can override `prepare_arguments` in the Model like this:

```
package Blog::Model::Filesytem;
# generated code here
sub prepare_arguments {
    my ($self, $app) = @_;
    return { base => $app->{base} };
}
```

Now the adapted `Filesystem` Model will work exactly like the one we made earlier, but with very little Catalyst-specific code.

If you are writing a Model that needs a new backend class to be created every time you call `$c->model` or once per request (instead of once per application), you can use the `Catalyst::Model::Factory` and `Catalyst::Model::Factory::PerRequest` modules included with `Catalyst::Model::Adaptor`. They are all used in the same way (as above, substituting `Factory` or `Factory::PerRequest` for `Adaptor`), but integrate your backend class with Catalyst in slightly different ways. For most cases, these Models will be all you need.

# Other Components

Models are just the tip of the iceberg—Views and Controllers work the same way (and implement the same methods) as Models. You can easily create custom Views and Controllers and inherit from them in your application to improve the reusability of your application's code.

# Summary

In this chapter, we looked at alternate ways to access the data model. We first added the ability to execute raw SQL to a standard `DBIC` model, and contrasted the code with normal `DBIC` resultset access. Then, we completely eliminated `DBIC` and wrote a database Model that used `DBI` to run raw SQL on the database. Next, we created a Filesystem Model from scratch, and learned how to use `COMPONENT` and `ACCEPT_CONTEXT` to integrate the Model with the Catalyst application. We also saw how using `Catalyst::Model::Adaptor` made writing a maintainable Model easier.

# 7
# Hot Web Topics

Traditionally, web applications were lonely and isolated. They each had their own set of users and data, and never acknowledged the existence of other applications. Today, things are changing. Web applications provide public APIs so that other applications can programmatically interact with their data and users. Users can visit sites and later request that the site notifies them when it has been updated.

Another new development is widespread adoption of dynamic JavaScript-enabled web applications. Gone are the days of slow waits between pages while things loaded; AJAX allows web applications to be almost as responsive as native desktop applications. In this chapter, we'll take a look at how to get your Catalyst application in on the fun! We'll add a REST API to allow other programs to easily access our application. Then, we'll use this API to add AJAX interactivity to our application. Finally, we'll modify our mini-blog application to allow users to subscribe to the latest posts.

## REST

A feature that many public websites are beginning to offer their users is the ability to get the information out of the application through a well-defined API (Application Programming Interface). Instead of forcing users to "screen-scrape" the HTML (programmatically parsing the pages that normal browser-based visitors see on the screen), which is tedious and prone to error, the application provides developers with the ability to access the application's entities in a serialized (XML, JSON, etc.) format. Thanks to a wide variety of data deserializers for nearly every programming language, getting data from a web application into your application is extremely easy to implement and maintain with this approach.

There are two main methods of providing this functionality; RPC (Remote Procedure Call), like XML-RPC or SOAP (Simple Object Access Protocol) and REST (Representational State Transfer). RPC-based approaches create an "RPC endpoint" URL for your application and clients send requests (like *give me address 42* or *delete person 10*) to this URL and get responses back. All requests use the same endpoint.

REST uses a cleaner approach; it provides a URL for each entity ("noun") and the client uses HTTP verbs to operate on these. Instead of sending an HTTP `GET` request to `/address/42/delete` to delete address 42, we send an HTTP `DELETE` to `/address/42`. A `GET` request to that location would return the serialized address and a PUT request would update the data with the serialized version sent with the request. POST-ing to the `/address` URL will create a new address.

In addition, all errors (and status indication) that can arise during this process are returned as standard HTTP codes. If an address isn't found, the REST interface returns *404 Not Found*. When an entity is created, the server returns *201 Created* along with the serialized entity. If a certain HTTP method doesn't make sense for a certain entity, *405 Method Not Allowed* is returned. There's no strict standard dictating what to return when, but the convention is to pick the most descriptive HTTP status code. The idea is to make it as easy as possible for an off-the-shelf HTTP client to understand what the response means.

We'll see all of this in action as we add a REST interface to our `AddressBook` application.

# Getting some REST

In this section, we'll add REST to the `AddressBook` application so that API clients can easily look up people and their addresses. We'll write a simple command-line client for accessing this interface, and we'll use it in the next section to implement an interactive JavaScript interface.

The first step is to install Catalyst's REST plug-in; `Catalyst::Controller::REST`. `Catalyst::Controller::REST` is a controller base class that will handle most of the REST details for us. It will automatically determine the type of incoming data and deserialize it into a Perl object. When we send a response, it will automatically serialize the response entity into the format that the client requested. It also adds some convenience functions, so we don't have to remember the proper HTTP response codes for each operation. Finally, it includes an ActionClass that will dispatch different HTTP methods to different Perl methods. We'll make use of all these features when creating the REST interface.

## REST Controller

To provide a clean namespace for our REST actions, we're going to implement the REST interface in a separate controller called "REST". Let's start by creating `/lib/AddressBook/Controller/REST.pm`:

```
package AddressBook::Controller::REST;
use strict;
use warnings;
use base qw(Catalyst::Controller::REST);

__PACKAGE__->config->{serialize}{default} = 'JSON';
1;
```

This creates the basic controller, and sets the default serialization method to JSON (JavaScript Object Notation). Clients can override this by sending a standard HTTP Accept: header. They specify the format that their `PUT` or `POST` request is in by setting a Content-type: header. Formats supported by `Catalyst::Controller::REST` include JSON, YAML, XML, raw PHP, raw Perl, FreezeThaw and Storable. Refer to the documentation for a full list and what headers to send for each type.

## REST Authentication

Before we write any more code, we need to think about how to handle authentication for the REST interface. As users of the API will most likely not be using a browser, requiring them to log in, get a cookie and send it with each request would be cumbersome. As a result, REST (and RPC) interfaces usually use some other sort of authentication.

The most common method (used by Flickr and Google, among many others) is to give each user an "API key". The API key works like a username and password, but can be disabled if the user abuses the API (without disabling his normal web access). The API key is sent in the headers of every request and the REST interface verifies it before performing the request.

As it seems unlikely that anyone would abuse our `AddressBook's` API, we'll just send the normal username and password with every request. Since there's no standard HTTP header for this, we'll use X-Username and X-Password.

In addition, we'll want the REST interface to work (partially) from a web browser, so we will also check to see if a user is logged in through the normal cookie method. If he is, we won't bother checking for the X-Username and X-Password headers.

Every REST request will need to be authenticated, so we'll add the authentication check in the begin method of the REST controller as follows:

```
sub begin : ActionClass('Deserialize') {
    my ($self, $c) = @_;

    my $username = $c->req->header('X-Username');
    my $password = $c->req->header('X-Password');

    # require either logged in user, or correct user+pass in headers
    if ( !$c->user && !$c->login($username, $password) ){
        # login failed
        $c->res->status(403); # forbidden
        $c->res->body("You are not authorized to use the REST API.");
        $c->detach;
    }
}
```

Note that we are also applying the `Deserialize ActionClass` here. Normally the REST controller deserializes the request automatically, but we're overriding it's begin method where it would perform this task. So, we re-add it explicitly so that everything continues to work normally.

We also need to tell our normal ACL plug-in to ignore the REST area, so at the bottom of AddressBook.pm, we add:

```
__PACKAGE__->allow_access('/rest'); # rest does its own auth
```

## Adding an Entity

Now that our interface is protected appropriately, we can start adding some entities. The format for implementing REST entities with `Catalyst::Controller::REST` is as follows. We first create a standard Catalyst action that acts as the entity (noun). We use the normal `:Local`, `:Global`, `:Path`, etc. attributes to map the Action to a URL. However, we also add the REST ActionClass to the Action. This ActionClass will eliminate some tedium associated with REST. Instead of a chain of if statements like the following:

```
if   ($c->req->method eq 'GET') { handle GET  request }
elsif($c->req->method eq 'POST'){ handle POST request }
elsif( ... ) ...
else { return an error }
```

we can write the following:

```
sub entity :Local :ActionClass('REST'){
   # do some setup for each request
}
sub entity_GET  { handle GET  request }
sub entity_POST { handle POST request }
```

Catalyst will take care of returning an HTTP error code when a method isn't implemented, and will also allow an HTTP client to ask what methods are implemented for a given entity.

Let us apply this by creating the shell of a person entity as follows:

```
sub person :Local :ActionClass('REST') {
    my ($self, $c, $id) = @_;
    $c->stash(id => $id);
}

sub person_GET {
    my ($self, $c) = @_;
    my $id = $c->stash->{id};

    my $person = $c->model('AddressDB::People')->
                                    find({id => $id});

    if ($person) {
        $self->status_ok($c, entity =>
                              mk_person_entity($person));
    }
    else {
        $self->status_not_found($c, message =>
                                  'No matching person found');
    }
}

sub mk_person_entity {
    my $person = shift;
    my $addresses =
      [ map {
          mk_address_entity($_)->{address}
        }
        $person->addresses
      ];
```

```
        return { person =>  { firstname => $person->firstname,
                              lastname  => $person->lastname,
                              fullname  => $person->name,
                              id        => $person->id,
                              addresses => $addresses,
                            }
               };
    }
```

Here, we create the main person action, which optionally accepts an ID number, and implements the `GET` method. Notice that we use some convenience methods in `Catalyst::Controller::REST` to handle the HTTP plumbing for us. When a record is found successfully, we call `status_ok` with the entity. When a record is not found, we call `status_not_found` with an error message. These two methods will send the appropriate HTTP response codes (*200* and *404*, respectively) and will serialize the provided entity and error message with the client's serializer of choice.

One thing to watch out for is that we don't implement the `mk_address_entity` method until later in the chapter. So for testing purposes, comment out the `map {}` statement and the `address => $addresses` hash entry for now.

Once you've added this code, you're ready to test your first REST action! Start the dev server, open a web browser and point it to `http://localhost:3000/rest/person/1`. Depending on what headers your browser sends, you'll either see an XML version of the person object:

```
<opt>
       <data id="1" name="person" firstname="Jonathan"
        fullname="Jonathan Rockway" lastname="Rockway" />
</opt>
```

or perhaps a YAML version:

```
---
person:
  firstname: Jonathan
  fullname: Jonathan Rockway
  id: 1
  lastname: Rockway
```

And if your browser sends no Accept header at all, you'll see the JSON fallback:

```
{"person":{"firstname":"Jonathan","lastname":"Rockway","id":1,"fulname:"J
onathan Rockway"}}
```

As you can see, regardless of the format returned, the information is much easier to reuse than it would be without the API.

Now that we have the basic idea of REST, let's add a `PUT` method for updating the existing records:

```
sub person_PUT {
    my ($self, $c) = @_;

    my $id = $c->stash->{id};
    my $person = $c->model('AddressDB::People')->
                                  find_or_new({id => $id});

    if ($person) {
        $person->firstname ($c->req->data->{firstname})
          if $c->req->data->{firstname};

        $person->lastname  ($c->req->data->{lastname} )
          if $c->req->data->{lastname};

        $person->insert_or_update;

        $self->status_created($c,
                                 entity   =>
                                    mk_person_entity($person),
                                 location =>
                                   $c->
                                    uri_for("/rest/person/$id"));
    }
    else {
        $self->status_not_found($c,
              message => 'No matching person found');
    }
}
```

This looks similar to `GET`, but we actually update the record with data from the serialized request (available via `$c->request->data`). When we update the record successfully, we return a *201 Created* response. By convention, we include the URL where this object can be requested, but we also include the object so that the client doesn't have to make another request. REST is flexible; you can use both a location and an entity, or just one of them.

> We're not doing any data validation here (other than not changing fields that aren't sent). In a real application, you'll want to factor the validation code out of the Person controller (and into the Model, usually) and share it between the REST and non-REST interface. When the data is invalid, simply return a *400 Bad Request*, which tells the client to not repeat the request without changing the data.

With `PUT` done, we need a way to create a new record (without providing an ID). `POST` serves this purpose:

```
sub person_POST {
    my ($self, $c) = @_;
    my $person = $c->model('AddressDB::People')->
      create({ firstname => $c->req->data->{firstname},
               lastname  => $c->req->data->{lastname},
             });
    my $id = $person->id;
    $self->status_created($c,
                          entity   =>
                             mk_person_entity($person),
                          location =>
                             $c->uri_for("/rest/person/$id"));
}
```

Finally, we need a way to delete records:

```
sub person_DELETE {
    my ($self, $c) = @_;
    my $id = $c->stash->{id};
    my $person = $c->model('AddressDB::People')->
          find({id => $id});

    if ($person) {
        $self->status_ok($c,
                         entity => mk_person_entity($person));
        $person->delete;
    }
    else {
        $self->status_not_found($c,
                   message => 'No matching person found');
    }
}
```

In this example, we return a copy of the deleted object, but this isn't always necessary. It's perfectly fine for the `DELETE` method to delete the object and just return *200 OK*.

With the person entity out of the way, let us add an interface to the address objects. The procedure is exactly the same:

```
sub address : Local : ActionClass('REST'){
    my ($self, $c, $id) = @_;
    $c->stash(id => $id);
}

sub address_GET {
    my ($self, $c) = @_;
    my $id = $c->stash->{id};
    my $address = $c->model('AddressDB::Addresses')->find({id =>
                                                 $id});
    if ($address) {
        $self->status_ok($c, entity => mk_address_entity($address));
    }
    else {
        $self->status_not_found($c, message => 'No matching address
                                                found');
    }
}
sub address_PUT {
    my ($self, $c) = @_;
    my $id = $c->stash->{id};

    eval {
        my $address = $c->model('AddressDB::Addresses')->
          find_or_new({id => $id});

        $address->location($c->req->data->{location})
          if $c->req->data->{location};

        $address->postal   ($c->req->data->{postal})
          if $c->req->data->{postal};

        $address->phone    ($c->req->data->{phone})
          if $c->req->data->{phone};

        $address->email    ($c->req->data->{email})
          if $c->req->data->{email};
```

```
        $address->person  ($c->req->data->{person})
          if $c->req->data->{person};

        $address->insert_or_update;

        $id = $address->id;
        $self->status_created($c,
                        entity   => mk_address_entity($address),
                        location => $c->uri_for("/rest/address/$id"));

    };
    if ($@) {
        $self->status_bad_request($c,
                             message => "Invalid data supplied: $@");

    }
}

sub address_POST {
    my ($self, $c) = @_;

    eval {
        my $address = $c->model('AddressDB::Addresses')->
          create({ location => $c->req->data->{location},
                   postal   => $c->req->data->{postal},
                   phone    => $c->req->data->{phone},
                   email    => $c->req->data->{email},
                   person   => $c->req->data->{person},
                 });
        my $id = $address->id;
        $self->status_created($c,
                        entity   => mk_address_entity($address),
                        location => $c->uri_for("/rest/address/$id"));
    };
    if ($@) {
        $self->status_bad_request($c,
                        message => "Invalid data supplied: $@");
    }
}

sub address_DELETE {
    my ($self, $c) = @_;
    my $id = $c->stash->{id};
```

```
    my $address = $c->model('AddressDB::Addresses')->find({id =>
$id});

    if ($address) {
        $self->status_ok($c, entity => mk_address_entity($address));
        $address->delete;
    }
    else {
        $self->status_not_found($c, message => 'No matching address
found');
    }
}

sub mk_address_entity {
    my $address = shift;

    return { address => { id          => $address->id,
                          person      => $address->person->id,
                          person_name => $address->person->name,
                          email       => $address->email,
                          phone       => $address->phone,
                          postal      => $address->postal,
                          location    => $address->location,
                        }
           };
}
```

Now that you have the `mk_address_entity` function, you can return the address records for a person when the person is requested i.e. you can remove the comments from the earlier lines.

This time we're doing a bit of validation. As the database might throw an exception when a foreign key or *NOT NULL* constraint is violated, we wrap database writes in an `eval {}` block. If there's a database error, we return *400 Bad Request* and the error message from the database. You'll probably want to return a more detailed error message in a real application, as your users probably don't care about what database constraints you have.

# REST Easy

That's all there is to creating an API for your application—give each object a URL and allow HTTP verbs as actions to perform on that object.

In the next section, we'll use our own REST API to implement AJAX.

# AJAX

AJAX is a technique for dynamically adding new data to a web page that's already loaded. It technically stands for **Asynchronous JavaScript And XML**, but the original meaning has been diluted such that AJAX also refers to **Synchronous JavaScript And JSON**, as well. Think of it as DHTML that can dynamically retrieve data from the server in the background.

As JavaScript has matured greatly over the last few years and browser support is generally solid, there's no reason to shy away from its use. A little JavaScript can greatly improve the user experience for users that choose to enable it.

In this section, we'll improve the `AddressBook` user interface a bit by adding some AJAX. The end goal is to be able to edit addresses "in place". Instead of clicking "edit" and waiting for the address editing page to load, the text fields will turn into text boxes and the user can begin editing immediately. When he's done, clicking submit will submit the address for validation and the process will proceed as usual.

## Getting Started

The bulk of AJAX is getting the data from the server to the client in JSON or XML form. However, handling the JSON data on the client side is where most of the effort is spent. There are several frameworks that do this and they all work fine with Catalyst. Some of the most popular are Dojo, jQuery, mootools, and prototype. Prototype is popular (and even has a Catalyst plug-in), but it's hard to integrate with other JavaScript, so it's best to avoid it for maintainability reasons. The other frameworks have more features and cause fewer undesirable side effects.

For our application, we're going to take a more Perl-y approach and use a framework called *Jemplate*. Jemplate is basically Template Toolkit for JavaScript. You send your TT template to the client along with some JSON, and the client will render it and update the web page accordingly. I prefer this approach because I can reuse my TT templates and my REST interface. (Other frameworks require that you send HTML back, so you have to write completely new Actions and templates to satisfy them.)

### Jemplate

Jemplate is actually a two-part framework. Half of it is the TT to JavaScript complier, which runs inside our application. The other half is the JavaScript that runs in the client's browser. To get the Catalyst part, simply install `Catalyst::View::Jemplate` from `CPAN`. Then, run the following command line:

```
$ perl script/addressbook_create.pl view Jemplate Jemplate
```

Next, create `root/jemplate` where the jemplates will live and edit the `INCLUDE_PATH` in `AddressBook::View::HTML` to look like the following:

```
__PACKAGE__->config({
    ...
    INCLUDE_PATH => [
        AddressBook->path_to( 'root', 'jemplate'),
        AddressBook->path_to( 'root', 'src' ),
        AddressBook->path_to( 'root', 'lib' ),
    ],
    ...
});
```

This will allow TT to access the jemplates.

Continuing, we need to create an Action in the Root controller that will compile all the jemplates in the jemplate directory and send the JavaScript to the browser. (This sounds inefficient, but compilation only happens once and both the server and client will cache the compiled results.)

In `lib/AddressBook/Controller/Root.pm`, add the following:

```
=head2 jemplate

Return the jemplates.

=cut

sub jemplate : Global {
    my($self, $c) = @_;
    $c->forward('View::Jemplate');
}
```

This will make the jemplate JavaScript available at `/jemplate`.

Lastly, we need to add a Cache backend to the application so that we can cache the compiled jemplates. Install `Catalyst::Plugin::Cache::Store::FastMmap` from the `CPAN` and then add `Cache` and `Cache::Store::FastMmap` to the `use Catalyst` line where you load the other plug-ins. Also, add the following configuration somewhere before `__PACKAGE__->setup`:

```
__PACKAGE__->config->{cache}{expires} = 43200;
__PACKAGE__->config->{cache}{backends}{jemplate}{store} = 'FastMmap';
__PACKAGE__->config->{'View::Jemplate'}{jemplate_dir} =
  __PACKAGE__->path_to('root', 'jemplate');
__PACKAGE__->config->{'View::Jemplate'}{jemplate_ext} = '.tt2';
```

This sets up a Jemplate cache, shared between all instances of your application, using the `FastMmap` backend. We also configure the Jemplate compiler to treat `*.tt2` in `root/jemplates` as jemplates to compile and send to the client.

The final step is to generate the Jemplate runtime JavaScript

```
$ jemplate --runtime > root/static/Jemplate.js
```

and include it on every page by editing `root/lib/site/html` and adding the following lines in the `<head>` section:

```
<script type="text/javascript"
        src="[% base %]static/Jemplate.js"></script>
<script type="text/javascript"
        src="[% base %]jemplate"></script>
```

We're also including the compiled jemplates, even though we haven't written any as yet. You only need that one line of JavaScript to include all the jemplates in the `jemplate` directory.

# Implementing AJAX

Now that we've set up the Jemplate framework, we can start writing jemplates.

The basic workflow goes like this:

1. Create an action that supplies JSON to the client.
2. Write a Template Toolkit template to turn the JSON into HTML.

The syntax for a Jemplate is the same as a regular template; if your JSON action returns a structure like `{hello:world}`, then you can access `hello` with the `[% hello %]` syntax in the template. (Arrays and hashes work too; Jemplate is similar to Template Toolkit.) After that, you need to call Jemplate's process function on the client side with the filename of the template to use, the URL where the JSON can be fetched from and the ID of the HTML DOM element to be replaced with the rendered text.

We'll see this in action by implementing the in-place address editor described earlier.

The first step is to create a Jemplate that will render an address' JSON (or Catalyst stash entry) as either an editable form or as a view-only piece of text. We'll use the view-only part to initially populate the view via TT, and then show the editable form via AJAX when requested. The same TT template will run on both the server and the client, which is the real power of Jemplate.

The template will be called `edit_address.tt2` and will live in the `root/jemplate` directory:

```
[% IF error %]
 <p class="error">[% error %]</p>
[% END %]
[% IF view_only %]
<b>[% address.location | html  %]</b>
<a href="[% Catalyst.uri_for("/address/edit/$address.id") %]"
   onclick="show_address_edit_form([% address.id | html %]); return
false;">
Edit</a>
<a href="[% Catalyst.uri_for("/address/delete/$address.id") %]">
Delete</a>
<br />
<div class="address" id="address_[% address.id | html %]">
  <address>[% address.postal | html | html_line_break %]</address>
  Phone: [% address.phone | html %]<br />
  Email: [% address.email | html %]<br />
</div>
[% ELSE %]
<form name="edit_address" method="post"
      action="../address/edit/[% address.id %]">
<input name="_" type="hidden" value="_" />
<input id="_submitted_address_edit" name="_submitted_address_edit"
       type="hidden" value="1" />
<table>
<tr>
  <td>Location</td>
  <td><input name="location"
            type="text" value="[% address.location | html %]" /></td>
</tr>
<tr valign="top">
  <td>Mailing Address</td>
  <td><textarea cols="60" name="postal" rows="4">[% address.postal |
html %]</textarea></td>
</tr>
<tr valign="top">
  <td>Phone Number</td>
  <td><input name="phone" type="text"
            value="[% address.phone | html %]" /></td>
</tr>
<tr valign="top">
  <td>E-Mail Address</td>
  <td><input name="email" type="text" value="[% address.email %]" /></
td>
</tr>
<tr valign="top">
  <td align="center" colspan="2"><input name="_submit" type="submit"
```

```
value="Submit" /></td>
</tr>
</table>
</form>
[% END %]
```

The HTML inside the form is copied from the FormBuilder output; we're going to trick FormBuilder into thinking that this is just a regular FormBuilder form so that we don't have to reimplement validation, etc. (If the AJAX-submitted form is invalid, the user will just get the regular FormBuilder address editor page.)

As this template is mostly duplicating the functionality in `root/src/address_fragment.tt2`, we'll edit that file to just include the Jemplate:

```
[% INCLUDE "edit_address.tt2" view_only = 1 %]
```

You should be able to start the server now and navigate to the list of people and addresses. It should look exactly the same as before, as we haven't really changed anything yet. We only moved the `address_fragment` code into the `edit_address` template. We haven't added any JavaScript interactivity yet; everything is static HTML rendered by TT on the server.

Now let's add the interactivity. The basic idea is to make the `edit` link for each address call the Jemplate process function instead of navigating to another page. We'll leave the href attribute of the link intact, though, so that users without JavaScript will not be affected. The basic pattern for this is:

```
<a href="non-javascript" onclick="function(); return false">
```

The `return false` tells the browser to not follow the `href` after the JavaScript function runs.

Now all that's left is to write that `function()`. As we're going to have multiple addresses on the same page, the function should only operate on a specific ID. When run, it should request the address data from `/rest/address/id` and render the template into a `#address_id div`. The code that does that looks like this:

```
function show_address_edit_form(id) {
   Jemplate.process('edit_address.tt2',
              '[% Catalyst.uri_for("/rest/address/") %]'+id,
              '#address_'+id);
 }
```

That function should be placed in `root/lib/site/html`, in the `<head>` section, surrounded by `<script type="text/javascript"></script>` tags.

When we were editing the edit_address.tt2 Jemplate earlier, we changed the link to run that JavaScript function (for the correct ID). That's all we needed to do; everything is in place for the in-place editor to work. Start the server, navigate to the list of addresses, and click edit. The text of the address should be replaced with an editable form! That's AJAX.

If it's not working for you, you might want to try installing Firefox and the Firebug extension. Firebug will show you all JavaScript errors and AJAX requests (requests and responses with complete headers) and will let you set JavaScript breakpoints. If something's wrong with the JavaScript, Firebug should help you identify the problem very quickly.

If you have that part working, let's add one more feature; the ability to cancel editing. All this feature does is request the Jemplate again, but with editing disabled.

First we need to modify the edit_address Jemplate to have another div to install the read-only version back into. Before the:

```
<b>[% address.location | html %]
```

line, add a wrapper div:

```
<div id="outside_address_[% address.id | html %]">
```

Also be sure to close that div with a </div> tag, just before the [% ELSE %] directive. At the very bottom of the file (or where your designer prefers), add a simple link:

```
<a href="#"
   onclick="cancel_address_edit([% address.id | html %]);
                                                  return false">
  [X] Cancel edit
</a>
```

This is the link that will appear in the edit mode to allow the user to cancel the edit. Now, let us implement the cancel_address_edit function, which goes in the same place as the show_address_edit_form function:

```
function cancel_address_edit(id){
  var data = Ajax.get('[%
                    Catalyst.uri_for("/rest/address/") %]'
                       +id);
  data = JSON.parse(data);
  data.view_only = 1;
  var elem = document.getElementById('outside_address_'+id);
  Jemplate.process('edit_address.tt2', data, elem);
}
```

We have to do the JSON parsing "manually" this time, because we want to set view_only to a true value before we let Jemplate render the template.

To be sure the new version of the Jemplate takes effect, `rm -rf /tmp/addressbook` and restart the server. You should now be able to cancel the edit operation by clicking the link. Using the same template on both the client and the server is a powerful concept, and should make it easy for you to quickly implement a JavaScript-based user interface.

We can see a rendered in-place edit form, firebug on the lower half of the figure showing AJAX response below:

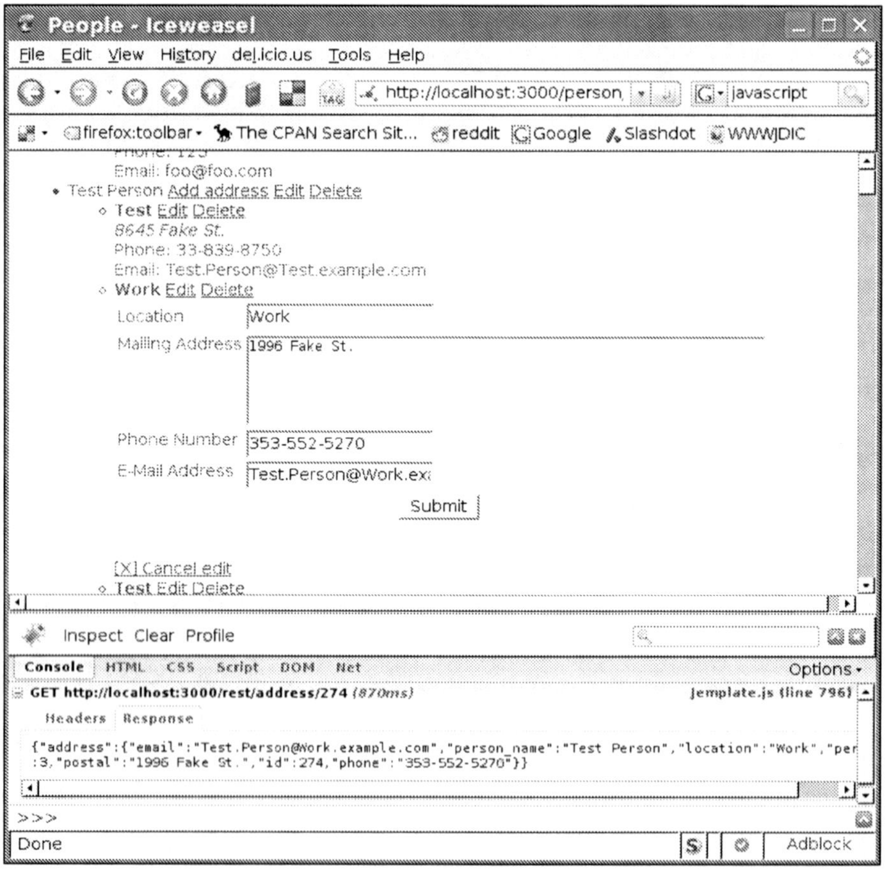

The cancelled in-place edit is seen in the following figure:

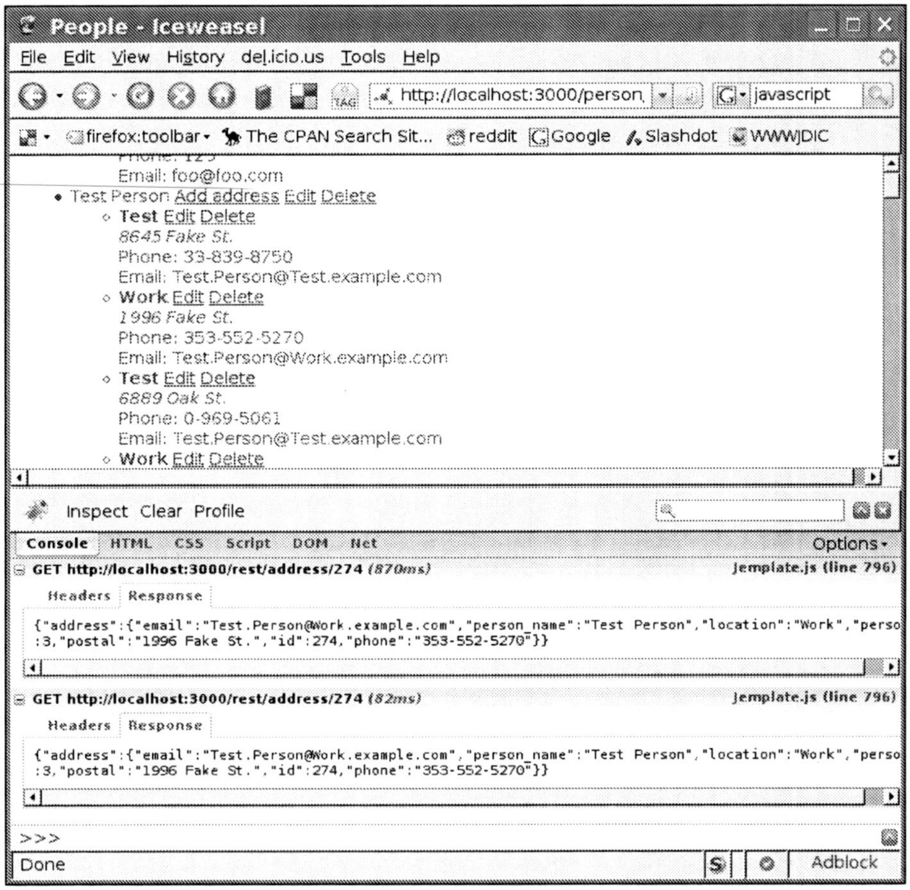

# RSS

The final topic that we'll examine is RSS feeds. An RSS feed is an XML format designed to let users subscribe to website and receive notification whenever a new article (or other piece of content) is posted. It works best for news sites or blogs.

RSS is beginning to be phased out in favor of Atom, which serves the same purpose but is an actual IETF standard. Users use RSS and Atom interchangeably and most RSS readers support Atom feeds. We'll be using the `XML::Feed` `CPAN` module to generate the RSS feed, which can generate Atom and legacy RSS from the same code.

To demonstrate the concept of RSS, we'll add an RSS feed to our mini-blog program from Chapter 6. To start, let's create a Controller to generate RSS feeds. As the RSS feed is specific to one piece of data and no templating system is used to generate the Feed, we're going to do everything inside a controller. If your application has multiple sources of data that you want to create a View that converts the stash to an RSS feed, instead.

Here's the source of the Feeds controller (in `Blog/lib/Blog/Controller/Feeds.pm`):

```
package Blog::Controller::Feeds;
use strict;
use warnings;
use base 'Catalyst::Controller';
use XML::Feed;
use DateTime;
sub atom : Local {
    my ($self, $c) = @_;
    $c->stash->{type} = 'Atom';
}
sub rss : Local {
    my ($self, $c) = @_;
    $c->stash->{type} = 'RSS';
}
sub end : Private {
    my ($self, $c) = @_;
    my @posts = $c->model('Filesystem')->get_recent_posts;
    my $feed = XML::Feed->new($c->stash->{type});
    $feed->title("Test Blog Feed");
    $feed->link($c->uri_for('/'));
    $feed->description("Test feed for my mini-blog");
    $feed->author("Your Name");
    $feed->language('en-US');
    foreach my $post (@posts) {
        my $entry = XML::Feed::Entry->new($c->stash->{type});
        $entry->title($post->title);
        $entry->content($post->body);
        $entry->issued(DateTime->from_epoch(epoch => $post->created));
        $entry->modified(DateTime->from_epoch(epoch =>
          $post->modified));
        # entry unique ID
        $entry->link($c->req->base.$post->created.$post->title);
```

```
            $feed->add_entry($entry);
        }

        $c->res->content_type('application/xml');
        $c->res->body($feed->as_xml);
    }
    1;
```

Creating an RSS feed is very simple. The first two actions let the user select what type of feed he wants based on the URL. Regardless of his choice, we forward to end Action where we actually render the feed.

Here, we create an `XML::Feed` object and then set as many attributes as possible (the manual for `XML::Feed` shows the whole list of possible attributes). Then, for each blog post, we create an `XML::Feed::Entry`, populate it and add it to the feed. At the very end, we send the generated XML to the user.

When a user subscribes to the feed, his client will request the feed every few hours. When a new article is added (as specified by "link", the article's unique id), he'll be alerted that the site has changed. Most users prefer that the full text of the updated article be in the "content" field in the RSS entry (so they can view the article right inside the RSS reader), but it's acceptable to only include the first paragraph so the user will visit your site for the full story.

# Summary

In this chapter, we developed a REST API to allow easy access to our application's data. We used this API to ease development of an interactive JavaScript interface to editing addresses. Finally, we added an RSS feed to our mini-Blog to allow users to subscribe to the latest updates and posts.

# 8
# Testing

Automatic testing is an important part of any programming project. It's always good to know that your application works correctly, but it's tedious to manually click through your application's interface every time you change something. Automatic testing transfers this burden onto the computer—after you've written the tests, the application will test itself whenever necessary. This makes adding new features a low risk operation; because your tests will start failing as soon as you break something, you'll be able to fix the problem immediately, and you won't have to worry about the fix breaking something else. If your tests are well-written, you can spend your time adding features, not tracking down obscure bugs at 3 A.M.

While this book doesn't intend to push any development methodology, there are a few schools of thinking on when to write tests. One is called "Test Driven Development", which suggests that you always write tests before you write any code. The idea is that before adding a feature you run your test suite, notice that everything passes, and then add some failing tests. Then you write the code until the tests *go green*, and you repeat the process for the next feature. When all the features are implemented, you also have a fully tested application, as no code can be written without writing a test first. This is an easy way to ensure that all of your code is tested; you're simply not allowed to implement a feature until it's tested. You won't have to worry about not having enough time to test something before release—if the feature is working, it's also tested. This is generally good, which is why the movement has attracted so much positive attention.

On the other end, the spectrum is waiting until your application is completely built before you write tests. Although it looks like we're doing this in the book, I actually wrote the tests along with the code but saved them up until this chapter so that they would get enough text to explain them adequately. I don't recommend that you try this for your real applications. Writing tests is a development aid, so waiting until development is complete misses much of the point of testing. The tests will be helpful for the next development cycle, but you, still probably wasted a lot of time in *this* cycle manually doing what the computer could do for you. So get disciplined and write tests as you develop the code the first time. Even though it seems like do actually you're wasting time not writing application code, you'll find that in the end you save time, and you won't lose sleep wondering what your last commit broke.

I prefer a hybrid approach to writing tests. I try to write as many tests as possible for a component or feature before I start writing a code for it, but I don't take any effort to make sure I got every case that I'm going to write the code for. Then I code for a bit, and test the basic flow of the application through the interface, just to make sure I didn't do anything too stupid (typos, etc.) Once I'm sure that the application doesn't contain any obvious errors, I write tests for the corner cases, and fix the errors in the code without using the interface at all. If a bug comes up later, I'll experiment a bit to reproduce the bug, add a test to the appropriate error, and then try to make the test pass without wasting time with the web interface.

As you get familiar with testing, you'll find a style that works well for you. If this chapter is your first exposure to automated testing, I recommend that you try the "Test Driven Development" methodology. After a while, you'll know when you don't need to strictly adhere to the procedure, but in the mean time, you'll be writing tested code at a pretty good pace.

In this chapter, we'll take a look at the technologies and techniques available to make testing your Catalyst application easy. We'll start by seeing how to run the auto-generated tests, and where to put new ones. Then we'll begin testing `ChatStat` by testing the data model outside of Catalyst. After that, we'll write a few tests to ensure that the web interface is nicely working with the data model. Then we'll write some tests for the Address Book application.

# Mechanics

Before we start writing tests, let's take a look at what we have so far. Out of the box, your Catalyst application already has a few tests in the `t/` directory of the application. You can run these by making a `Makefile` with `Makefile.PL` as follows:

```
$ perl Makefile.PL
<output>
$ make test
t/01app.................ok
t/02pod.................skipped
        all skipped: set TEST_POD to enable this test
t/03podcoverage.........skipped
        all skipped: set TEST_POD to enable this test
t/controller_Address....ok
```

```
t/controller_Person.....ok
t/model_AddressDB.......ok
t/view_Jemplate.........ok
All tests successful, 2 tests skipped.
Files=7, Tests=9,  3 wallclock secs ( 2.92 cusr +  0.29 csys =  3.21 CPU)
```

The tests you see running here were added by `catalyst.pl` (the ones that start with numbers), or by the `addressbook_create.pl` script (the ones that start with model and view). These tests don't really do much testing, because they're just auto-generated tests that see if the code compiles. Here's what the `t/view_Jemplate.t` looks like:

```
use strict;
use warnings;
use Test::More tests => 1;
BEGIN { use_ok 'AddressBook::View::Jemplate' }
```

Although this test doesn't do much, it does show the structure of a test file. A test is just a Perl script that ends with a `.t` extension. We use strict and use warnings, and then use a module called `Test::More`. `Test::More`, which produces an output that can be read by a module called `Test::Harness`. This is what `make test` uses to generate the summary above. If you run the tests manually, the output looks like the following:

```
$ perl -Ilib t/view_Jemplate.t
1..1
ok 1 - use AddressBook::View::Jemplate;
```

This output format is called **TAP** (Test Anything Protocol), and is generated for you by `Test::More`. Although you could generate TAP manually, it's easier to just let the module do it for you.

One last note—`Perl` comes with a command called `prove` that will do the same thing as `make test`:

```
$ prove -Ilib t/view_Jemplate.t
t/view_Jemplate....ok
All tests successful.
Files=1, Tests=1,  0 wallclock secs ( 0.20 cusr +  0.02 csys =  0.22 CPU)
```

`prove` is nice when you only want to run a few test files instead of the entire suite.

# Testing ChatStat

Now that we have seen what tests look like and how to run them, let's dive into testing ChatStat. When I was first writing ChatStat, I designed it with testability in mind. The key practice here is to make as many components of the application work without depending on other parts of the application. Testing a Perl class is very easy, but firing up a Catalyst application and testing it by making requests and looking at the HTML is hard. So, I tried to keep the need for the second type of test down by not doing much inside Catalyst. All the hard stuff is inside the easily testable Perl modules. This not only makes testing easy, it's just a plain good design. Without any effort on my part, I can use the same code to write a command-line version of the app, or perhaps an IRC interface.

Let's get started by writing some tests for the ChatStat message parser. This isn't particularly related to the Catalyst part of the application, but if this doesn't work, the whole app is useless. In addition, this is the simplest test to write, so it's a good practice before we move on to more complex parts of the application.

We'll start with a very simple test for the parse_nickname function, located in the ChatStat::Robot::Parser module from Chapter 5. This function takes a string like person!~username@some-host.com and produces an array like ['person', 'username', 'some-host.com'].

In t/irc-parser-nickname.t, add the following:

```
use strict;
use warnings;
use Test::More;
use ChatStat::Robot::Parser;
my %tests =
   (
    # me @ example.com
    'jrockway!~jrockway@example.com' =>
           ['jrockway', 'jrockway', 'example.com']
   );
plan tests => scalar keys %tests;
while (my ($k, $v) = each %tests) {
    my $get    = [parse_nickname($k)];
    my $expect = $v;
    is_deeply($get, $expect, "$k parses");
}
```

We wrote this test by creating a table at the top of the test with the input string and the expected output result. Then we told `Test::More` how many tests we're going to run (so it can warn us if the test file dies halfway through), and finally we run `parse_nickname` on each input and used the `is_deeply` function in `Test::More` to see if the "got" and "expected" data was the same.

You can try running the test with `prove` as follows:

```
$ prove -Ilib t/irc-parser-nickname.t
t/irc-parser-nickname....ok
All tests successful.
Files=1, Tests=1,  0 wallclock secs ( 0.12 cusr +  0.00 csys =  0.12 CPU)
```

The advantage of writing a test in this table-driven format is that you can add another assertion (test case) without writing any more code. If you append another test case to the `%tests` hash:

```
my %tests =
  (
   # me @ example.com
   'jrockway!~jrockway@example.com' =>
         ['jrockway', 'jrockway', 'example.com'],
   'another!~test@some-place.com' =>
         ['another', 'test', 'some-place.com'],
  );
```

You'll now see two tests running:

```
$ prove -Ilib t/irc-parser-nickname.t
t/irc-parser-nickname....ok
All tests successful.
Files=1, Tests=2,  0 wallclock secs ( 0.07 cusr +  0.01 csys =  0.08 CPU)
```

You can take this technique a step further and write test cases in a separate (non-Perl) file and load that file as the `%tests` hash. Then you can have someone other than a programmer write your test cases. If you do choose to follow this route, you should take a look at FIT (`http://fit.c2.com/`), and the `Test::FITesque` module on CPAN.

# Testing a Database

`ChatStat` is a pretty database-heavy application, so there's no way to avoid testing the database part. We can make testing the database less painful by providing an easy way for creating an empty database just for testing. This is easy to do with SQLite; we just create a temporary database, deploy our schema to it, run the tests and then delete the database. Whenever I start a database application, I create a small module to automate this. For `ChatStat`, it's called `ChatStat::Test::Database`, and looks like the following:

```
package ChatStat::Test::Database;
use strict;
use warnings;
use Directory::Scratch;
use base 'ChatStat::Schema';
sub connect {
    my $class = shift;
    # setup temp space
    my $tmp = Directory::Scratch->new;
    my $db  = $tmp->touch('database');
    # "connect" to temp database; deploy schema
    my $schema = $class->SUPER::connect("DBI:SQLite:$db");
    $schema->deploy;
    # done!
    return $schema;
}
```

All we do here is subclass our real `DBIx::Class` schema, and change the connect method to create a temporary database first. The `Directory::Scratch` module handles the management of the temporary scratch space, so we don't need to worry about cleaning up when we're done with tests.

Now we're ready to write database tests. The simplest thing to test would be the `everything` ResultSet, which will take "opinion" records and coalesce them into a ranked list of "things" with their point values. For example, given the input "test++, test--, foo++, foo++, bar--, and baz+-", we should get output like "foo => 2, baz => 0, test => 0, bar => -1".

Now that we know what we're testing (and have some sample data), we just need to have the computer check it for us. Let's create `t/schema-report-everything.t`:

```
use strict;
use warnings;
use Test::More tests => 1;
use ChatStat::Test::Database;
use ChatStat::Robot::Action;
my @RECORDS = ([qw/test  1/],
               [qw/test -1/],
               [qw/foo   1/],
               [qw/foo   1/],
```

```
                [qw/bar  -1/],
                [qw/baz   0/],
               );
my @EXPECT  = ([qw/foo   2/],
                [qw/baz   0/],
                [qw/test  0/],
                [qw/bar  -1/],
               );
my $schema  = ChatStat::Test::Database->connect;
$schema->record(ChatStat::Robot::Action->
                new({ who     => 'foo!~foo@test.com',
                      word    => $_->[0],
                      points  => $_->[1],
                      channel => '#test',
                      reason  => 'test',
                      message => 'test',
                    }))
  for @RECORDS;
my @everything = map {[ $_->thing, $_->total_points ]}
  $schema->resultset('Things')->all;
is_deeply [sort {$a->[0] cmp $b->[0]} @everything],
          [sort {$a->[0] cmp $b->[0]} @EXPECT],
          'got expected everything';
```

With the database abstracted away, writing this test is easy. We start by defining our input data and output data. Then we connect to the database and add the input data to the database via `ChatStat::Robot::Action`. Then we run our `everything` report and see that it matches the expected data.

This is all that's there to testing. There are some other tests for other reports in `ChatStat` included with the book's source code, but they're not much different than the above test. They simply add data to the database, and see if the results of queries make sense.

# Testing the Web Interface

Once you're confident that the backend is well-tested, you need to make sure that the Catalyst part of your application is working smoothly. We have some more tools at our disposal for this task, `Catalyst::Test` and `Test::WWW::Mechanize::Catalyst`.

The basic idea here is to use `Catalyst::Test` (or similar) to make requests against the application and then see if the response contains the data we're looking for. (You can also do other things, like test if the HTML is valid, etc.)

As we still need the database, we'll have to jump through a few hoops to get a real Catalyst application to use the temporary database. What we need to do is to create the testing database and then create a Catalyst `config` file that tells Catalyst to use the test database instead of the real one.

Here's the code for a module that does that, `Chatstat::Test::Database::Live`:

```
package ChatStat::Test::Database::Live;
use strict;
use warnings;
use ChatStat::Schema;
use Directory::Scratch;
use YAML qw(DumpFile);
use FindBin qw($Bin);
use base 'Exporter';
our @EXPORT = qw/schema/;
my $schema;
my $config;
BEGIN {
    my $tmp = Directory::Scratch->new;

    my $dsn = "DBI:SQLite:$db";
    $schema = ChatStat::Schema->connect($dsn);
    $schema->deploy;
    $config = "$Bin/../chatstat_local.yml";
    DumpFile($config, {'Model::DBIC' => {connect_info => [$dsn]}});
}
sub schema { $schema };
END { unlink $config };
```

When you use this module, it will create a test database, connect to it and write a "local" `config` file, with the connection information pointing to the test database. After this module is loaded and Catalyst is started, it will see the `config` file with the suffix `_local` and override the existing `config` file with the data contained in the local file. The `END{}` block will delete the local `config` file when the test is done running, so you won't have to worry about the local configuration cluttering up your disk.

Now that we have a test database shared between the `test` script and the Catalyst app, we can start writing some tests. Let's test the page at `/things`, which list's every thing that has an entry in the database.

We'll start by creating the basic test file called `t/app-live-everything.t` as follows:

```
use strict;
use warnings;
use Test::More tests => 3;
use ChatStat::Robot::Action;
use ChatStat::Test::Database::Live;
use Test::WWW::Mechanize::Catalyst qw/ChatStat/;
my $schema = schema();
my $mech = Test::WWW::Mechanize::Catalyst->new;
# test empty page
is_deeply [$schema->resultset('Things')->everything], [], 'no things
yet';
$mech->get_ok('http://localhost/things/');
$mech->content_unlike(qr/test/);
```

This will create the database, and then use `Test::WWW::Mechanize::Catalyst` to start an instance of the application. Then we get the test database and a `Test::WWW::Mechanize` object (that runs requests against our app instead of the Internet).

With the setup done, we make sure there are no `things` in the database yet, and that they don't show up on the page. The `$mech->get_ok` method will run the `/things/` action in our application (the localhost in the URL means "our application" in this case, not the web server running on the local host). The `$mech->content_unlike` looks for a regex on the page, and is a passing test if the regex doesn't match. In this case, we're looking to ensure that the word "test" doesn't show up on the page yet. We'll add it to the page right before the next test; this is just a sanity check to make sure it doesn't show up there for some other reason.

Now, let's add "test++" to the database, and see if the page updates correctly. First, let's add a little utility to make inserting "test++" into the database easy:

```
sub add_opinion {
    $schema->record(ChatStat::Robot::Action->
                    new({ who     => 'foo!~foo@test.com',
                          word    => $_[0],
                          points  => $_[1],
                          channel => '#test',
                          reason  => 'test',
                          message => 'test',
                        })
                   );
}
```

I add this to the very bottom of the test file so that I don't have to skip past it when reading the tests.

After the existing tests, add the following:

```
# add an opinion
add_opinion(test => 1);
my @things = $schema->resultset('Things')->everything->all;
is $things[0]->total_points, 1, 'got 1 point';
is $things[0]->thing, 'test', 'for test';

$mech->get_ok('http://localhost/things/');
$mech->content_like(qr/test/);
$mech->content_like(qr/1/);
```

And be sure to change the test counter at the top of the test to 8, since we just added five more assertions.

These test cases look like the ones above. We add a piece of data to the database, check that it's in the resultset, and then see if the correct text appears on the web page. To complete this test, let's add some negative and zero entries, and make sure those work:

```
add_opinion(foo => 0);
$mech->get_ok('http://localhost/things/');
$mech->content_like(qr/foo/, 'foo shows up, even though it has 0 
points');

add_opinion(test => -1);
add_opinion(test => -1);
$mech->get_ok('http://localhost/things/');
$mech->content_like(qr/negative/, q{now there's a negative entry});
$mech->content_unlike(qr/positive/, q{but no more positives});

add_opinion(bar => 1);
$mech->get_ok('http://localhost/things/');
$mech->content_like(qr/positive/, q{positive is back});
$mech->content_like(qr/bar/, q{and bar shows up});
```

That's all we need for this test. After running this, you can be pretty sure that adding opinions to the database is reflected in the web interface.

You can do many more things with `Test::WWW::Mechanize::Catalyst`. If you're looking for documentation, be sure to see the docs for `Test::WWW::Mechanize`, `WWW::Mechanize`, and `LWP::UserAgent`, since that's the inheritance hierarchy for `Test::WWW::Mechanize::Catalyst`. Anything that those modules can do, `Test::WWW::Mechanize::Catalyst` can do against your Catalyst application.

# Testing the Address Book

Testing the Address Book requires some techniques that we didn't need for `ChatStat`. Most of the `AddressBook` is hidden behind a login screen, so we'll have to log in in order to test the app. It also requires us to fill out a lot of forms. Finally, it has a JavaScript interface that we can't test without a live web browser. In this section, we'll see how to test those parts of the application.

## Logging In

We'll start by adding a test database module to `AddressBook`. This is almost an exact copy of the one we created for `ChatStat`, but we add a convenience function for creating a test user and logging in as that user:

```
package AddressBook::Test::Database::Live;
use strict;
use warnings;
use AddressBook::Schema::AddressDB;
use Directory::Scratch;
use YAML qw(DumpFile);
use FindBin qw($Bin);
use base 'Exporter';
our @EXPORT = qw/log_in schema/;
my $schema;
my $config;
BEGIN {
    my $tmp = Directory::Scratch->new;
    my $db  = $tmp->touch('db');
    my $dsn = "DBI:SQLite:$db";
    $schema = AddressBook::Schema::AddressDB->connect($dsn);
    $schema->deploy;
    $config = "$Bin/../addressbook_local.yml";
    DumpFile($config, {'Model::AddressDB' => {connect_info =>
[$dsn]}});
}
sub schema { $schema };
sub log_in { # counts as 4 tests
    my $mech = shift;
    my $person = schema()->
      resultset('People')->create({ firstname => 'Test',
                                    lastname  => 'User',
                                  });
```

```
    my $user = schema()->resultset('User')->
      create({ username => 'test_user',
               password => 'ABCDEFGHI',
               person   => $person,
             });
    $mech->get_ok('http://localhost/login');
    $mech->form_name('login');
    $mech->field(username => 'test_user');
    $mech->field(password => 'ABCDEFGHI');
    $mech->click('_submit');
    $mech->content_like(qr/Logged in successfully/);
    $mech->content_like(qr/Logged in as/);
    $mech->content_like(qr/Test User/);
    return $user;
}
END { unlink $config };
1;
```

The important part of this module is the `log_in` function. It creates a test user and uses Mechanize's form functionality to visit the log in page, enter the username and password, "click" submit and check that the user logged in successfully.

Now it's easy to start writing tests. Let's start by testing the login and logout functionality in a file called `t/live-login.t` as follows:

```
use strict;
use warnings;
use Test::More tests => 7;
use AddressBook::Test::Database::Live;
use Test::WWW::Mechanize::Catalyst 'AddressBook';
my $schema = schema();
my $mech   = Test::WWW::Mechanize::Catalyst->new;
log_in($mech);
$mech->follow_link_ok({url_regex => qr/logout/},
                      'follow logout link');
$mech->content_like(qr/Not logged in/);
$mech->content_unlike(qr/Test User/);
```

All we do here is create the `schema` and `mech` objects, try to log in (which is 4 assertions) and then try to log out. It's important to note that Mechanize is just like a regular web browser, and cookies and sessions are preserved. (There are even back, forward, and reload "buttons" that `Mech` can "click".)

# Testing Forms

Now that we have a logged in user, let's try creating a person, then adding an address for him. To get started, let's add the standard header to `t/live-add-person.t` as follows:

```
use strict;
use warnings;
use Test::More tests => 17;
use AddressBook::Test::Database::Live;
use Test::WWW::Mechanize::Catalyst 'AddressBook';
my $schema = schema();
my $mech   = Test::WWW::Mechanize::Catalyst->new;
```

We'll continue by adding the user that `log_in` creates to the editor and viewer roles, so the ACL rules don't prevent the test from running:

```
# give user a role that lets him edit
my $user = log_in($mech); # 4 tests
my $viewer = $schema->resultset('Role')->create({ role => 'editor' });
my $editor = $schema->resultset('Role')->create({ role => 'viewer' });
$schema->resultset('UserRole')->create({ user => $user->id,
                                         role => $editor->id });
$schema->resultset('UserRole')->create({ user => $user->id,
                                         role => $viewer->id });
```

Now the test user can access and edit any part of the application. Let's try adding a new Person by clicking links and filling out forms:

```
# now try adding a new person
$mech->get_ok('http://localhost/');
$mech->follow_link_ok({ text => 'Add a new person' });
$mech->content_like(qr/Adding a new person/, 'on the add person
page');
$mech->form_number(1); # first form
$mech->field(firstname => 'Avery');
$mech->field(lastname  => 'Newperson');
$mech->click('_submit');
$mech->content_like(qr/Added Avery Newperson/, 'added a very new
person');
```

Now there should be a new person, `Avery Newperson`, in the database. Let's retrieve a `Person` record from the database to make sure that the interface is actually updating the database:

```
# find ID of new person
my $person = $schema->resultset('People')->
  find(qw/Avery Newperson/, { key => 'name' });
my $id = $person->id;
ok $person->id > 0, 'got a person';
```

Now that we have the ID, let's add a Home address for `Avery`:

```
# add an address
$mech->get_ok("http://localhost/address/add/$id");
$mech->content_like(qr/Adding a new address \s* for Avery Newperson/);
$mech->form_number(1);
$mech->field(location => 'Home');
$mech->field(postal   => 'This is the postal address.');
$mech->field(phone    => '123-456-7890');
$mech->field(email    => 'test@example.com');
$mech->click('_submit');
$mech->content_like(qr/Added new address for Avery Newperson/);
$mech->content_like(qr/This is the postal address[.]/);
```

If that worked, the `$person` above should now have some related addresses as follows:

```
# see if that's in the database
my $address = $person->search_related('addresses')->first;
is $address->postal, 'This is the postal address.';
my $aid = $address->id;
```

Let's conclude by deleting the address as follows:

```
# now delete the address
$mech->follow_link_ok({url_regex => qr{address/delete/$aid} },
                      'blow away address');
$mech->content_like(qr/Deleted Avery Newperson's Home address/);
$mech->content_unlike(qr/This is the postal address[.]/);
```

Now you can run the test with make test or prove:

```
$ prove -Ilib t/live-add-person.t
t/live-add-person....ok
All tests successful.
Files=1, Tests=17,  2 wallclock secs ( 1.68 cusr +  0.08 csys =  1.76
CPU)
```

What used to be a few seconds of clicking through the interface manually is now an automatic test that can tell you whether your application works in just a few seconds. For a real application, you'll want to test everything, but this test is a good start. Good tests will include tests of common cases but also edge cases. For example, if a field requires a number, what happens if the user enters "0 but true" (not a number) or "0e0" (a number)? Edge cases are where bugs show up, so try to be tricky and eliminate them in development. It's much more fun to fix a bug that a test finds as opposed to one that causes your site to go down at 3 in the morning.

As an aside, if you'd like to have your tests written automatically, you can install a CPAN module called `HTTP::Recorder`. `HTTP::Recorder`, which will act as a proxy between your application and the browser, and will translate any clicks and form submissions into code that you can paste into your Mechanize-based test. It's good for recording activity during user testing. If someone runs into a bug, you'll have a detailed log of what they clicked. You can copy that into your test file, add some assertions and you'll be able to fix the bug without having the user click through the interface to find the bug again.

# Testing JavaScript

The last remaining part of the Address Book to test is the Jemplate-based in-place address editor. To test this, we'll use a tool called Selenium RC (`http://www.openqa.org/`) to run tests directly in the browser. Selenium is a tool that sits between your application, the test script, and the web browser. The test script sends the Selenium server commands to run inside the web browser. The web browser then executes those commands, and returns the results to the Selenium server and then your test script.

It can be hard to get it up and running because it requires the Java Runtime Environment and a working web browser. It is somewhat experimental, and the author has only tested on Cygwin with Firefox and IE and Debian GNU/Linux with Firefox.

Developing Selenium tests is pretty easy, thanks to the Selenium IDE Firefox extension available at `http://www.openqa.org/selenium-ide/`. It turns Firefox into an IDE that can record and edit tests, and save them to the Perl format.
To create a test against the Catalyst application, we'll start by recording the basic outline of the test with Selenium IDE.

To get started, start the Address Book application, then open the IDE and click the red record button. Then enter `http://localhost:3000/` in the address bar and wait for the page to load. Log in as the test user, navigate to the list of all addresses, click the first edit link to edit the address in place and then change each of the fields to a new value. Click on `submit` to store the changes, and then highlight all the text you just entered (now as part of the static page), right-click and select "`verifyTextPresent`" for each field.

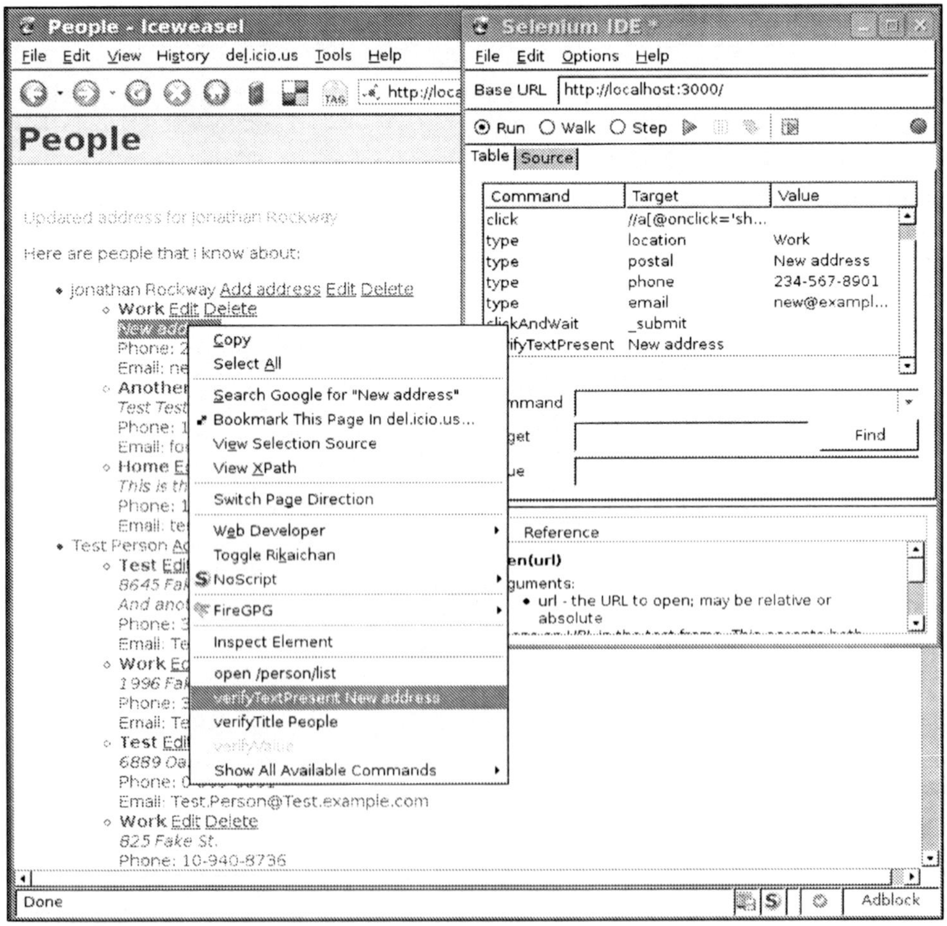

You should now have a Selenium test that looks like the following:

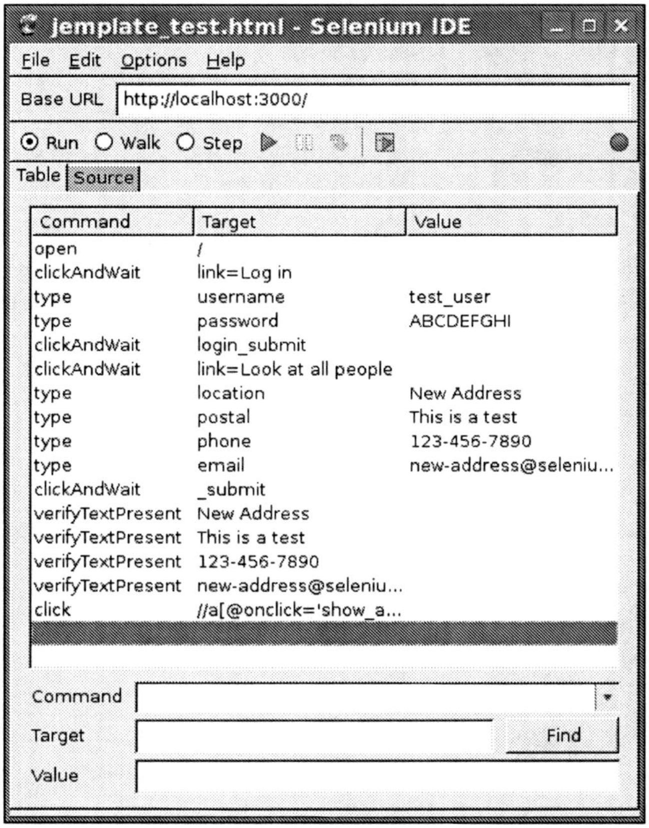


Now you can select all the records, change the clipboard format to Perl, and copy-and-paste the result into into `t/selenium-edit.t`. We're going to edit the result a bit, though.

Here's what you get right out of the Selenium IDE:

```
$sel->open_ok("/");
$sel->click_ok("link=Log in");
$sel->wait_for_page_to_load_ok("30000");
$sel->type_ok("username", "test_user");
$sel->type_ok("password", "ABCDEFGHI");
$sel->click_ok("login_submit");
$sel->wait_for_page_to_load_ok("30000");
$sel->click_ok("link=Look at all people");
$sel->wait_for_page_to_load_ok("30000");
$sel->type_ok("location", "New Address");
$sel->type_ok("postal", "This is a test");
$sel->type_ok("phone", "123-456-7890");
```

```
$sel->type_ok("email", "new-address\@selenium.example.com");
$sel->click_ok("_submit");
$sel->wait_for_page_to_load_ok("30000");
$sel->is_text_present_ok("New Address");
$sel->is_text_present_ok("This is a test");
$sel->is_text_present_ok("123-456-7890");
$sel->is_text_present_ok("new-address\@selenium.example.com");
$sel->click_ok("//a[\@onclick='show_address_edit_form(6); return
false;']");
```

To make this test run exactly as in the IDE, you just need to use `Test::WWW::Selenium::Catalyst` by adding something like this to the top of the file:

```
use strict;
use warnings;
use Test::More tests => 20;
use AddressBook::Test::Database::Live;
use Test::WWW::Selenium::Catalyst 'AddressBook';
my $sel = Test::WWW::Selenium::Catalyst->start;
```

There are still a few tweaks we need to make the test work. We need to replace the hard-coded 6 with the ID of a sample address we create. We'll start by creating the necessary database records right before we create the `$sel` object:

```
my $person = schema()->
  resultset('People')->create({ firstname => 'Test',
                                lastname  => 'User',
                              });
my $user = schema()->resultset('User')->
  create({ username => 'test_user',
           password => 'ABCDEFGHI',
           person   => $person,
         });
my $address = schema()->resultset('Addresses')->
  create({ person => $person->id,
           location => 'Home',
           postal => 'Postal address.',
           phone => 'Phone',
           email => 'email@email.com',
         });
my $aid = $address->id;
```

Then you just need to replace the 6 on the last line with `$aid`. As soon as you do that, you should be able to run the test from `prove`. A web browser window will pop up and run the actions that your test script dictates. If everything goes well, you should see the *All tests successful.* message at the very end. After it's working, you should add some more tests to see that the database was modified as you expected it to be.

If all doesn't go well, take a look at the manual page for `Test::WWW::Selenium::Catalyst`.

Once it's up and running, though, you should find it a valuable testing tool, especially as the Selenium IDE makes it easy for anyone to record test cases.

Selenium isn't the only way to test JavaScript. You can also write `Test::More` style tests in JavaScript by using the `Test.Simple` module from the JSAN (the JavaScript version of the CPAN).Check it out at `http://openjsan.org/doc/t/th/theory/Test/Simple/0.21/`.

# Summary

In this chapter, we learned how to write programs to test our Catalyst application automatically. We saw how to test the individual non-Catalyst components, and then saw how to test the components inside Catalyst with `Test::WWW::Mechanize::Catalyst`. We then learned how to test form-heavy applications with Mechanize, and finally how to test the JavaScript components with Selenium. Testing was once a tedious manual chore, but now the computer can do it for you!

# 9

# Deployment

At some point in your application's life cycle, you're going to want to run the application on a machine other than your development environment. In this chapter, we'll cover packaging your application (for internal or CPAN release) and running that package in a production environment with a real web server.

## Basics

The first step in deploying your application is to copy your application from your development/build environment to your production environment. This may sound trivial, but it's important to make sure that your process is easy and repeatable. If you require every step to be done manually, it's likely that at some point (under the pressure of short maintenance windows), something will be missed and your users will be unhappy. Are you sure you remembered to install every dependency, update the source tree on every server in the farm, change permissions and edit configuration files appropriately?

Fortunately, Catalyst makes it easy to do deployment right. If you've been diligent about keeping the dependencies in your `Makefile.PL` up to date, you'll find it very easy to manage dependencies and the application itself.

Let's start with a quick run through of the `Makefile.PL` build process. We will use `Makefile.PL` twice, once on the build system (to build the package) and again on the target system, to build the application itself.

The first step is to run `Makefile.PL` on your development or build system:

```
$ perl Makefile.PL
```

This will generate a `Makefile` that includes some useful targets; `make dist`, `make test`, `make clean`, `make manifest`, `make distclean` and many others. Before we build a distribution, we'll want to run `make distclean` to delete any non-code that has accumulated during the development process. Unfortunately, as the `Makefile` is considered a temporary file, it will be removed in this step. After the `distclean`, re-run `Makefile.PL` to regenerate the `Makefile`.

Now that you have a clean working directory, you can generate a "manifest" file containing a list of the files in your application. `make manifest` will do this automatically and save the results in a file called `MANIFEST`. If this file looks good, you're ready for the next step. If it contains entries that aren't a part of your application, then create a file called `MANIFEST.SKIP` to indicate paths to skip. A `MANIFEST.SKIP` that I usually use looks like this:

```
.git/
blib
pm_to_blib
MANIFEST.bak
MANIFEST.SKIP~
cover_db
Makefile$
Makefile.old$
```

The format is one regular expression per line. If a file's full path is matched by any regular expression in the file, it will be skipped over when building the manifest.

You can test the skip list by re-running `make manifest`. That command will inform you of what it added to, or removed from, the manifest based on the new skip rules.

When the manifest is to your liking, all that's left to do is to actually build the package with `make dist`. The `make dist` command will build a compressed `tar` file of your application called `MyApp-0.01.tar.gz` that contains the source (and `Makefile.PL`) of your application, suitable for uploading to the CPAN or copying to another system to install. The `0.01` in the file name is the version number, which can be changed by editing the `our $VERSION = '0.01'` line in your application's main file, `lib/MyApp.pm`. Traditionally, versions start at 0.01 and are increased by 0.01 on each release. Test releases are marked with a version number, an underscore and another number, like `0.01_01` (note that 0.01_01 sorts **after** 0.01). Many utilities assume this convention, so it's good to stick to it even if you don't plan to release your code to the world.

With this package built, the final step is to copy the tarball to your deployment server. On that machine, simply run:

```
$ tar xzvf MyApp-0.01.tar.gz
$ cd MyApp
$ perl Makefile.PL
$ make && make test
```

That will extract the application, generate the `Makefile`, install all the dependencies that `Makefile.PL` mentions and finally, run the application's automated test suite. If all goes well, you're ready to point your web server at the application directory.

# PAR Deployment

If your build environment and production are at the same platform, you can save some time and trouble by deploying a PAR package instead of manually building a tarball. A PAR file is a Perl Archive, a self-contained Perl application. It will contain your application and all the dependencies, which means that you can copy a single file to all of your production machines and have your application "Just Work".

Building a PAR is usually as simple as adding a line that says:

```
catalyst_par();
```

to your `Makefile.PL`, running `Makefile.PL`, and then running `make catalyst_par`. The PAR packer will examine your application to determine its dependencies and then generate an archive that bundles the dependencies, your application and the scripts to run the application together in a file called `myapp.par`. To run you application, put the par file somewhere convenient and then run `parl myapp.par <script>`, where the script is `myapp_server.pl`, `myapp_fastcgi.pl`, `myapp_test.pl`, etc. The PAR will unpack itself and then execute the requested command.

Note that the command is `parl`, not `Perl`; it's included in the `PAR` `CPAN` distribution, which must be installed on the target system.

Sometimes the auto-scanning of your application might not pick up all the dependencies; you can manually add a list of dependencies to always include by including:

```
catalyst_par_classes(qw/A::Dependency Another::Dependency .../);
```

inside `Makefile.PL`.

# Configuration Management

It's likely that your development and production environments will require different configuration files. Catalyst provides a few ways to handle this. The most flexible is to maintain separate configuration files for each instance of your application (development, staging, QA, production, etc.) and set the MYAPP_CONFIG environment variable to point to the correct file on each environment.

If there is a lot of configuration that overlaps between the instances, that approach might not be ideal. Catalyst has a concept of local configuration files that you can use instead. If there is an environment variable called MYAPP_CONFIG_LOCAL_SUFFIX set, then Catalyst will supplement the default configuration (say, myapp.yml) with a file named myapp_<suffix>.yml. The default suffix is local, so if you only have two environments to configure, you can put your development-specific settings in the local file and simply not copy the myapp_local.yml file to production.

If you have more than two environments, put the bulk of your config in myapp.yml, then create a myapp_envname.yml for each environment. Then just set the MYAPP_CONFIG_LOCAL_SUFFIX environment variable appropriately, and you're set.

> If you use the hostname as the suffix you can say MYAPP_CONFIG_LOCAL_SUFFIX='hostname'; then even the environment variable setting is identical between machines.

Alternatively, you can specify configuration directly as environment variables with the Catalyst::Plugin::ConfigLoader::Environment extension.

# Configuring a Web Server

Once you have your application working on the production machine, you're ready to point a real web server at it. Which server you use is usually decided by what your other applications are using. If you already have *Apache* and mod_perl set up, use that. If you aren't serving many users, you will probably be fine with just the development server included with Catalyst. If you're tired of Apache, you can use lighttpd with FastCGI. Catalyst tries to make mod_perl, FastCGI, and the development server behave the same, so you should use whatever is convenient for you. (Note that plain CGI is also an option, but it will be unbearably slow, so don't use it.)

Generally, new deployments are using Apache and FastCGI, since that configuration is relatively easy to set up and manage.

# Apache

Apache is the world's most common web server, so most sites are already using Apache and have a configuration that you can easily add your Catalyst app to. If you decide to use Apache, you can use either `mod_perl` or `FastCGI` to actually run your Catalyst application.

## FastCGI

FastCGI is easiest of the two to set up; simply install `mod_fastcgi` (or the newer `mod_fcgid`, which might be better for some users) and add the following to Apache's `httpd.conf`:

```
FastCgiServer /.../myapp/script/myapp_fastcgi.pl -processes 3
Alias /myapp/ /.../myapp/script/myapp_fastcgi.pl/
```

(Note that `...` above is an abbreviation for wherever you want your application code to live. Many sites use `/var/www` or `/var/www-apps`, but `/home/myapp/` or something similar is also possible.)

The above configuration will tell Apache to start (and maintain) three instances of your application, and to make the application available on the web under the `/myapp` URL. You can put the `Alias` directive inside a `VirtualHost` block to make your application available at the root of a virtual host.

If you'd like to run your `FastCGI` server on a separate machine, you can tell Apache about a `FastCGI` external server:

```
FastCgiExternalServer /var/www/htdocs/myapp.fcgi -host remote.server.
com:3010
Alias /myapp/ /var/www/htdocs/myapp.fcgi
```

Note that `/var/www/htdocs/myapp.fcgi` isn't a real file; it's a virtual file that ends with `.fcgi` (so Apache knows to invoke the `fastcgi-handler`) and exists inside the doc root (so Apache knows it's allowed to be served). The `-host` directive points `FastCGI` at the server running on `remote.server.com`, port `3010`.

On `remote.server.com`, you'll want to run `scripts/myapp_fastcgi.pl -l :3010` and setup firewall rules so that only your front end server can talk to port `3010`. You can also use another port number, as there is no defined standard port.

If your application is in a PAR, you can start an external `FastCGI` server by running `parl myapp.par myapp_fastcgi.pl -l :3010`. You can then configure a remote Apache with `FastCGI` to support to connect to that server, just as described above for the non-PAR case.

In addition, the external server need not be on another host, it can be run on localhost the same way. You can also use a named socket on the filesystem instead of a host and port; just say `-socket` instead of `-host`. It is easier to enforce permissions on files than TCP ports, so if you care about fine-grained access to the `FastCGI` server, you might like using the named socket better. Keep in mind that you can't use a named socket when the `FastCGI` server is running on a different host from the front-end web server.

# Static Content

One last tweak is to have Apache serve your static content without involving your Catalyst application. All you'll need to do is add an Alias directive like the following:

```
Alias /myapp/static /.../myapp/root/static
```

Apache can serve static content much more efficiently than your Catalyst application, so for maximum performance it's best to add this piece of configuration.

# mod_perl

For years, `mod_perl` was the only way to write efficient web applications, so it's still in wide use. Serving your Catalyst application with `mod_perl` is very easy. First, you'll need `Catalyst::Engine::Apache` from the CPAN.

Then, to a `mod_perl`-enabled Apache 2.x.x configuration, you'll just need to add:

```
PerlSwitches -I/.../myapp/lib
PerlModule MyApp
<Location /> # or you can use /myapp, or a VirtualHost, etc.
    SetHandler           modperl
    PerlResponseHandler MyApp
</Location>
```

On Apache 1.3, the setup is slightly different:

```
<Perl>
    use lib qw(/.../myapp/lib);
</Perl>
PerlModule MyApp
<Location />
    SetHandler perl-script
    PerlHandler MyApp
</Location>
```

Finally, if you're using PAR, you can install `Apache::PAR` and point Apache at the PAR instead of a directory:

```
PerlAddVar PARInclude /.../myapp.par
PerlModule Apache::PAR
PerlModule MyApp
```

These directives replace the `<Perl>` or `PerlSwitches` sections above (but not the `<Location>` section).

After you have setup your configuration, you can restart Apache and enjoy your app. The same static caveat with `FastCGI` applies to `mod_perl`, so you will want to add an Alias or Location for serving the static content directly. (This is more difficult with PAR, but you might want to take the slight performance hit for the convenience of one-file deployment. Additionally, you can copy the static content somewhere outside of the PAR file and only use the PAR for code. Then there is no performance hit, but maintenance is slightly more difficult.)

# Performance Considerations

Unfortunately, the `mod_perl` setup described above is not ideal. `mod_perl` works by loading your entire application into every Apache process. This means that when an Apache process has to spoon-feed a dial-up user a 200M movie (or 20k of HTML; the concept is the same), the memory that your application used is wasted streaming bytes instead of processing requests. On sites with high traffic, this will result in unacceptable performance, as the application processes will be tied up serving data (and you can't start more application processes because you'll be out of memory).

This is a well-known `mod_perl` problem not specific to Catalyst (or even Perl, `mod_ruby` and `mod_python` suffer the same problem), and is part of the reason why `FastCGI` is becoming popular.

The solution is to run a two-tiered architecture. In front of your `mod_perl` application processes, you place a lean load balancer (like perlbal) or a basic Apache process. The front end will pass dynamic requests to the backend application servers. When the dynamic result is ready, the dynamic server will send it very quickly to the front end server. The front end server will then send the response to the client. While that front end server is tied up, another lean front end server can dispatch another dynamic request to your application. This setup ensures that you are always using as much CPU and bandwidth as possible.

Setting up a front end server is covered in the mod_perl book at http://perl.apache.org/, and perlbal is covered in the next section. The only thing you need to do for Catalyst is to tell it that there's a frontend proxy by setting using_frontend_proxy to 1 in the application config. This option is necessary so that Catalyst will generate URLs that point to the front end server when you use uri_for.

If you're going to use mod_perl for a large site, be sure to set up a two-tiered architecture.

# Development Server and perlbal

The final deployment option is to simply use the myapp_server.pl development server. This server is not intrinsically limited in any way; you can expose it to the Internet and your application will work fine. The main problem is the same as mod_perl, though; feeding the resulting HTML (or images, etc.) back to the client will tie up system memory unnecessarily. Additionally, as the development server can only handle one connection at a time, users will have to wait in line to use your application, which is probably not acceptable unless your are creating something like a desktop web application.

That means, it's easy to get a very efficient two-tiered setup going with **perlbal**. The basic idea is to start a pool of development servers running on different ports, and then have perlbal load balance between them. perlbal will handle talking to clients and will send dynamic requests to a waiting development server. The performance of this setup will be excellent, as perlbal adds almost no overhead (it's used for popular sites like LiveJournal and Vox and easily handles hundreds of millions of requests a day).

To get started, install perlbal from the CPAN (it's also available at http://www.danga.com/perlbal/). Then, create a simple perlbal configuration file called /etc/perlbal/perlbal.conf that looks like this:

```
CREATE POOL myapp
  POOL myapp ADD 127.0.0.1:3010
  POOL myapp ADD 127.0.0.1:3011
  POOL myapp ADD 127.0.0.1:3012
  POOL myapp ADD 127.0.0.1:3013
CREATE SERVICE balancer
  SET listen          = 0.0.0.0:80
  SET role            = reverse_proxy
  SET pool            = myapp
  SET persist_client  = on
  SET persist_backend = on
ENABLE balancer
```

```
# open up a management port for dynamic configuration
CREATE SERVICE mgmt
  SET role   = management
  SET listen = 127.0.0.1:60000
ENABLE mgmt
```

When that's set up, start a few instances of your application:

```
$ perl script/myapp_server.pl -p 3010 -d
$ perl script/myapp_server.pl -p 3011 -d
$ perl script/myapp_server.pl -p 3012 -d
$ perl script/myapp_server.pl -p 3013 -d
```

and start perlbal:

```
$perlbal
```

Now visit `http://localhost/`, and you should be good to go. If you choose to keep perlbal's management interface up, you should firewall off its port (`60000`).

# Summary

In this chapter, we moved our application from development to production. We learned how `Makefile.PL` made it simple to manage dependencies and create packages. We also saw how to create a unique configuration for each environment, and how to set up a variety of web servers. Finally, we learned how to make our application a self-contained file, called a PAR.

# Index

## A

**address book, application**
address editing controller, adding 47-51
authentication 72
authentication, adding 75
authorization 73, 75
authorization, adding 75
Catalyst model, creating 33
configuration files 53
configuration files, using 54
configuring 55
controller, uses 41
CRUD 43
data, searching 64-70
database, accessing 33
database, schema files 34
database, sessions 59
database design 32, 33
database schema, creating in SQLite 32, 33
environment setup 32
forms 43-47
forms, building 44
people, viewing 40
People controller, creating 40, 42
relations, specifying 34
results, displaying 66
results, paging 67
resultset, displaying 67
Search Controller, creating 65
search form, generating 66
search page, generating 68, 69
search templates, creating 71
session engine 56
session plugin, loading 56
sessions 56, 57
sessions, adding 57, 58
sessions, modules 56
TTSite 37
**address book application, testing**
about 165
forums, testing 167, 168
JavaScript, testing 169-173
logging in 165, 166
**AJAX**
about 144
implementing 146-151
Jemplate 144
**Apache**
about 179
fastcgi 179
mod_perl 180
mod_perl, performance enhancing 181
mod_perl, serving Catalyst aplication 180
static content 180
**API key 135**
**application**
address book 31
deploying 175
skeleton 13
**Asynchronous JavaScript And XML.** *See* AJAX
**authentication**
about 72
application, configuring 77
guts, implementing 78
schema files, creating 76, 77
tables, creating in database 75
**authentication, REST**
about 135
API key 135
**Authentication plugin 72, 73**
**authorization**
about 73
implementing 81

## C

**Catalyst**
about 6
address book application 31
address book application, testing 165
application, building 31
application, deploying 175
application structure 18
authentication 72
authorization 72, 73
ChatStat application 83
ChatStat application, testing 158
configuration management 178
CPAN modules, creating 32
database model, creating 28
help 10
installing 9
installing from CPAN 9
mechanics 156, 157
model, creating 33
outside components, using 60-63
PAR, deploying 177
REST plugin, installing 134
ResultSet object, creating 29
skeleton application, creating 13, 14
skeleton application, debugging 14, 15
web server, configuring 178
**Catalyst application architecture**
about 6
extensibility 7
flexbility 8
reliability 8
reusability 8
**Catalyst model**
creating 127
**ChatStat application**
accessor, creating 86
building 83
data, extracting 92
data, putting on web 99-116
database, creating 84
database, populating 88-91
DBIC, chained ResultSets 95
DBIC, custom ResultSets 97
DBIC, features 93
DBIC schema, generating 85
running 107
tables, creating in SQLite 84
web interface, building 99
**ChatStat application, testing**
about 158, 159
database, testing 159-161
web interface, testing 161-164
**components**
Controller 6
Model 7
View 7, 20
**configuration management 178**
**CPAN**
Catalyst, installing from 9

## D

**database**
interface, understanding 34-36
**database, accessing ways**
Object-Relational Mapper 27
**database, skeleton application**
database model, creating 28
database model, using 29
database schema, creating 28
SQLite, installing 27
**database model**
creating 122, 123
**data putting on web, ChatStat application**
custom ResultSets, writing 104
macros, creating 100
main page 99
main page, writing 102, 103
ResultSets, adding 108
template, creating 101
**DBIC**
about 27
features 93
**DBIC model**
custom methods, implementing without raw SQL 121
database functions, calling 121, 122
extending 119
SQL, executing 120
**DBIx**
:Class. *See* DBIC
**development server**
about 182
perlbal 182

## F

**filesystem model**
blog application, creating 124, 125
creating 124
implementing 126
integrating, ACCEPT_CONTEXT used used 130
integrating, COMPONENT used 129
maintainable models, writing 130, 131
tweaking 128, 129

## I

**interface to database 34**

## J

**Jemplate, AJAX**
about 144-146
setting up 146
**JSON 144**

## M

**Makefile.PL**
about 175
running, on development system 175
**MyApp directory structure, skeleton application**
files in lib directory 18
files in MyApp directory 18
files in root directory 19
files in script directory 19
files in t directory 20

## O

**Object-Relational Mapper 27**

## P

**PAR**
deploying 177
**perlbal**
about 182
installing 182, 183

## R

**Representational State Transfer.** *See* **REST**
**REST**
about 133, 134
ActionClass 134, 136
adding, to address book application 134
authentication 135
controller, creating 135
entity, adding 136-143
**RSS feed**
about 151
adding, to mini-blog program 152
creating 152, 153

## S

**sessions 56**
**skeleton application**
creating 13
customizing 20
database, adding 27
MyApp directory structure 17
View, adding 21-23
View, technical details 26
**SQLite**
database schema, creating 32

## T

**testing**
address book application 165
ChatStat application 158
**TTSite**
about 37
index page, creating 38

## V

**View**
page rendering, template used 25, 26
Template Toolkit, rendering HTML pages 20

## W

**web server**
Apache 179
configuring 178

## Packt Open Source Project Royalties

When we sell a book written on an Open Source project, we pay a royalty directly to that project. Therefore by purchasing Catalyst: Accelerating Perl Web Application Development, Packt will have given some of the money received to the Catalyst project.

In the long term, we see ourselves and you—customers and readers of our books—as part of the Open Source ecosystem, providing sustainable revenue for the projects we publish on. Our aim at Packt is to establish publishing royalties as an essential part of the service and support a business model that sustains Open Source.

If you're working with an Open Source project that you would like us to publish on, and subsequently pay royalties to, please get in touch with us.

## Writing for Packt

We welcome all inquiries from people who are interested in authoring. Book proposals should be sent to `authors@packtpub.com`. If your book idea is still at an early stage and you would like to discuss it first before writing a formal book proposal, contact us; one of our commissioning editors will get in touch with you.

We're not just looking for published authors; if you have strong technical skills but no writing experience, our experienced editors can help you develop a writing career, or simply get some additional reward for your expertise.

## About Packt Publishing

Packt, pronounced 'packed', published its first book "Mastering phpMyAdmin for Effective MySQL Management" in April 2004 and subsequently continued to specialize in publishing highly focused books on specific technologies and solutions.

Our books and publications share the experiences of your fellow IT professionals in adapting and customizing today's systems, applications, and frameworks. Our solution-based books give you the knowledge and power to customize the software and technologies you're using to get the job done. Packt books are more specific and less general than the IT books you have seen in the past. Our unique business model allows us to bring you more focused information, giving you more of what you need to know, and less of what you don't.

Packt is a modern, yet unique publishing company, which focuses on producing quality, cutting-edge books for communities of developers, administrators, and newbies alike. For more information, please visit our website: `www.PacktPub.com`.

Printed in the United States
97929LV00005B/21-24/A